Developing Cross-Cultural Measurement

POCKET GUIDES TO
SOCIAL WORK RESEARCH METHODS

Series Editor
Tony Tripodi, DSW
Professor Emeritus, Ohio State University

Determining Sample Size
Balancing Power, Precision, and Practicality
Patrick Dattalo

Preparing Research Articles
Bruce A. Thyer

Systematic Reviews and Meta-Analysis
Julia H. Littell, Jacqueline Corcoran, and Vijayan Pillai

Historical Research
Elizabeth Ann Danto

Confirmatory Factor Analysis
Donna Harrington

Randomized Controlled Trials
Design and Implementation for
Community-Based Psychosocial Interventions
Phyllis Solomon, Mary M. Cavanaugh, and Jeffrey Draine

Needs Assessment
David Royse, Michele Staton-Tindall, Karen Badger,
and J. Matthew Webster

Multiple Regression with Discrete Dependent Variables
John G. Orme and Terri Combs-Orme

Developing Cross-Cultural Measurement
Thanh V. Tran

Intervention Research
Developing Social Programs
Mark W. Fraser, Jack M. Richman, Maeda J. Galinsky,
and Steven H. Day

THANH V. TRAN

Developing Cross-Cultural
Measurement

OXFORD
UNIVERSITY PRESS
2009

OXFORD
UNIVERSITY PRESS

Oxford University Press, Inc., publishes works that further
Oxford University's objective of excellence
in research, scholarship, and education.

Oxford   New York
Auckland   Cape Town   Dar es Salaam   Hong Kong   Karachi
Kuala Lumpur   Madrid   Melbourne   Mexico City   Nairobi
New Delhi   Shanghai   Taipei   Toronto

With offices in
Argentina   Austria   Brazil   Chile   Czech Republic   France   Greece
Guatemala   Hungary   Italy   Japan   Poland   Portugal   Singapore
South Korea   Switzerland   Thailand   Turkey   Ukraine   Vietnam

Copyright © 2009 by Oxford University Press, Inc.

Published by Oxford University Press, Inc.
198 Madison Avenue, New York, New York 10016

www.oup.com

Oxford is a registered trademark of Oxford University Press

Library of Congress Cataloging-in-Publication Data

Tran, Thanh V.
Developing cross-cultural measurement / Thanh V. Tran.
p.   cm. — (Pocket guides to social work research methods)
Includes bibliographical references and index.
ISBN 978-0-19-532508-9
1. Social work with minorities—United States—Methodology.
2. Cultural awareness—United States—Methodology.   I. Title.
HV3176.T714 2009
361.308'0973—dc22
2008037888

9 8 7 6 5 4 3 2 1

Printed in the United States of America
on acid-free paper

Preface

The United States historically has been a haven for immigrants and refugees from almost every corner of the globe. As the result, social workers have played a major role in helping the newcomers settle and adjust into their newly found communities. Cross-cultural issues are not new among those of us who are trained or identify ourselves as social workers. The profession of social work has a long tradition of advocating and serving clients from different cultural backgrounds (Lubove, 1965; Green, 1982). The question that remains to be answered is to what extent social workers are concerned about the impact of cultural differences in the implementation of services and the assessment of service outcomes across different social, economic, racial, and national groups. This small guide attempts to articulate the process of cross-cultural research instrument development in social work research and evaluation.

People migrate from place to place for different reasons, including the economy, political turmoil, religious persecution, war, and calamity. Immigration researchers often classify migration into two groups: the pulled and the pushed immigrants. Pulled immigrants migrate out of their country of origin by choice, and pushed immigrants migrate because of factors beyond their control. In addition, modern transportation technologies and the global economy have opened the borders of nations and continents, allowing more people to easily migrate across continents and nations. As reported by the United Nations, in 2002 there were approximately 175 million people living outside of the country of their birth. By the end of the twentieth century, with the explosion of information science and technology, people around the globe have been exposed to other cultures and are able to virtually and instantaneously connect with foreigners and strangers from every corner of the earth.

Changes in the U.S. immigration laws from 1965 to 1990 created opportunities for immigrants from diverse ethic/racial backgrounds to arrive in this country. In 1970, there were 10 million foreign-born individuals; this number increased to 14 million in 1980, 20 million in 1990, and by March 2000, the foreign-born population in the United States increased to 28 million (U.S. Census Bureau, 2000). Data from the 2000 U.S. Census also revealed that approximately 45 million (about 18%) people ages 5 years and older living the United States spoke a language other than English at home. More specifically, 10.5 million (about 23%) of these 45 million people either spoke no English or very little English (Li, McCardle, Clark, Kinsella & Berch, 2001). Indeed, the U.S. Census data also revealed that there were 11.9 million individuals considered "linguistically isolated," (Shin & Bruno, 2003). With demographic changes and the reality of cultural diversity in the United States and other parts of the world today, social work researchers are increasingly aware of the need to conduct cross-cultural research and evaluation, whether for hypothesis testing or outcome evaluation.

This book's aims are twofold: to provide an overview of issues and techniques relevant to the development of cross-cultural measures and to provide readers with a step-by-step approach to the assessment of cross-cultural equivalence of measurement properties. There is no discussion of statistical theory and principles underlying the statistical techniques presented in this book. The book draws information from existing cross-cultural research in the social sciences, public domain secondary data, and primary data from the author's research.

Chapter 1 provides the readers an overview of the definitions of culture, a brief discussion of cross-cultural research backgrounds in anthropology, psychology, sociology, and political Science, and the influences of these fields on social work.

Chapter 2 describes the process of cross-cultural instrument development from formulating the research aims to the assessment of cross-cultural measurement properties.

Chapter 3 discusses the preliminary tasks of a cross-cultural instrument development process. The chapter offers guides and recommendations for building a research support team for various critical tasks. Chapter 4 addresses the issues of adopting and adapting existing research instruments. The processes and issues of cross-cultural translation and assessment are presented and discussed in detail.

Chapter 5 is devoted to the process of developing new instruments. This chapter begins with a discussion of the foundation of measurement theories and the entire process of instrument development from the definitions of abstract concepts, the construction of observed indicators, and assessment of the validity and reliability of the new instruments.

Chapter 6 focuses on the analytical techniques to evaluate cross-cultural measurement equivalence. The chapter demonstrates the applications of item distribution analysis, internal consistency analysis, and exploratory factor analysis.

Chapter 7 explains and illustrates the application of confirmatory factor analysis and multisample confirmatory factor analysis to evaluate the factor structure and testing cross-cultural measurement invariance. Students will learn how to generate data for confirmatory factor analysis, presenting the results and explaining the statistical findings concerning measurement invariance.

Chapter 8 provides concluding remarks, makes recommendations for cross-cultural social work research, and offers some insight into the issues of treatment equivalence with respect to evidence-based social work in multicultural settings.

Although this book is prepared for social work audience in the United States, the issues of cross-cultural measurement equivalence and assessment techniques are applicable beyond any geographical locations.

Data Sources

Six data sets are used to provide examples throughout this book. The Chinese ($n = 177$), Russian ($n = 300$), and Vietnamese ($n = 339$) data were collected in the Greater Boston areas at various social service agencies and social and religious institutions. These self-administered surveys were conducted to study various aspects of health, mental health, and service utilization among these immigrant communities (Tran, Khatutsky,

Aroian, Balsam & Convey, 2000; Wu, Tran & Amjad (2004). This instrument was translated from English to Chinese, Russian, and Vietnamese by bilingual and bicultural social gerontologists, social service providers, and health and mental health professionals. The translations were also reviewed and evaluated by experts and prospective respondents to ensure cultural equivalence in the translations.

The Americans' Changing Lives Survey: Waves I, II, and III offers rich data for cross-cultural comparisons between African-Americans and Whites regarding important variables concerning physical health, psychological well-being, and cognitive functioning. This longitudinal survey contains information of 3,617 respondents ages 25 years and older in Wave I, 2,867 in Wave II, and 2,562 in Wave III (House, 2006).

The National Survey of Japanese Elderly (NSJE), 1987 has similar research variables as those used in the Americans' Changing Lives Survey. The purpose of this survey is to provide cross-cultural analyses of aging in the United States and Japan. The 1987 NSJE Survey contains data of 2,180 respondents ages 60 years and older (Liang & Maeda, 1997).

The 1988 National Survey of Hispanic Elderly people ages 65 years and older (Davis, 1997) was conducted to investigate specific problems, including their economic, health, and social status. The telephone survey was conducted in both Spanish and English. There were 937 Mexicans, 368 Puerto Rican-Americans, 714 Cuban-Americans, and 280 other Hispanics.

These data sets are used because they provide both micro- (within-nation) and macro- (between-nation) levels of cultural comparisons. The statistical results presented throughout the book are only for illustrations. Readers should not interpret the findings beyond this purpose.

Acknowledgments

I want to thank Dr. Tony Tripodi for inviting and encouraging me to work on this project. This book was initiated when I was director of the School of Social Work at California State University, Los Angeles. I appreciate the support from Boston College Graduate School of Social Work, Dean Alberto Godenzi, Dr. Ce Shen, the doctoral students who have taken SW953 at Boston College, and my family during the preparation of this publication.

Contents

Developing Cross-Cultural Measurement

1

Overview of Cross-Cultural Research

T his chapter discusses the concept of culture and reviews the basic principles of multidisciplinary cross-cultural research. The readers are introduced to cross-cultural research in anthropology, psychology, political science, and sociology. These cross-cultural research fields offer social work both theoretical and methodological resources. The readers will find that all cross-cultural research fields share the same concern—that is, the equivalence of research instruments. One cannot draw meaningful comparisons of behavioral problems, social values, or psychological status between or across different cultural groups in the absence of cross-culturally equivalent research instruments.

Definitions of Culture

Most of us are often fascinated with stories and tales from travelers who are fortunate and/or courageous to travel to unknown territories and encounter exotic cultures and people. Scholarly interests in cross-culture studies have their root in ancient Greece since the middle Ages (*see* Jahoda & Krewer, 1997; Marsella, Dubanoski, Hamada, & Morse, 2000). However, systematic studies of cultures originated from the field of anthropology. Edward Burnet Tyler (1832–1917) has been honored as the father of anthropology, and his well-known definition of culture also has been quoted numerous times in almost every major book and paper on studies of cultures. He views culture as "complex whole which includes knowledge, belief, art, morals, law, custom, and any other capabilities and habits acquired by man as a member of society" (Tyler, 1871, 1958). Since Tyler's definition of culture, there have been hundreds of definitions of culture by writers and scholars from different disciplines and fields. As noted by Chao & Moon (2005), culture is considered as one of the difficult and complex terms in the English language. This is also probably true in other languages. Even the United Nations Educational, Scientific and Cultural Organization (UNESCO) seems to have a problem with its definition of culture. UNESCO defines culture as the combination of literature and the arts, people's ways of life, societal value systems, traditions, and beliefs (http://portal.unesco.org/culture/). Kluckhohn (1954) defined culture as the memory of a society.

There have also been attempts to define culture by categorizing it into different types. As suggested by Barkow, Cosmides, and Tooby (1992), there are three types of cultures: metaculture, evoked culture, and epidemiological culture. Metaculture can be viewed as what makes human species different from other species. Evoked culture refers to the ways people live under different ecological conditions, and these ecological-based living conditions lead to within- and between-cultural differences known as epidemiological culture. The conceptualization of this cultural typology suggests reciprocal relationships between psychology and biology in the development of culture and society. Wedeen (2002) suggested a useful way to conceptualize culture as semiotic practices or the processes of meaning-making. Cultural symbols are inscribed in practices among societal members, and they influence how people behave in various social situations. For example, elder care-giving may have different symbolic meanings in different cultures and how members of a specific cultural practice their care-giving behaviors may have different consequences on the quality of life of the recipients. Generally, culture can be viewed as a combination of values, norms, institutions, and artifacts. Social values are desirable behaviors, manners, and attitudes that are for all members of a group or society to follow or behave. Norms are social controls that regulate group members' behaviors.

Institutions provide structures for society or community to function. Artifacts include all material products of human societies or groups.

All things considered, culture can be viewed as social markers that make people unique from each other based on their country of origin, race, or languages that they were born with. Although people are different because of their cultures, languages, races, religions, and other aspects, there are universal values and norms across human societies. The challenges of social work research are to investigate the similarities in the midst of obvious differences and diversity.

Multidisciplinary Perspectives of Cross-Cultural Research

Cultural Anthropology

Cultural anthropologists are pioneers in cross-cultural research and have influenced other cross-cultural research disciplines in the social sciences. Burton and White have suggested that cross-cultural research offers a fundamental component of meaningful generalizations about human societies (Burton & White, 1987). Cross-cultural anthropological research has encompassed several key variables or focuses across cultures or societies such as the roles of markets and labor, division of labor and production, warfare and conflicts, socialization and gender identity, reproductive rituals, households and polygyny, gender beliefs and behaviors, expressive behavior, technology, settlement pattern and demography, social and kinship organization, spirits and shamanism, and others (Burton & White, 1987; Jorgensen, 1979). The field of social anthropology can be divided into two schools: social anthropology studies involved in the comparative study of social structures and ethnology and comparative or historical cultural anthropology study cultures (Singer, 1968, p. 527). Two classic theories that have dominated the field of anthropology in the first half of the twentieth century are process–pattern theory (which emphasizes the analysis of cultural pattern) and structural–functional theory (which focuses on the study of cultural structure). Salzman (2001) reviewed and discussed four major theories that have guided cultural anthropology research, including functionalism, which emphasizes interconnection and mutual dependence among societal institutions or customs, and processualism, which focuses on the assumption that members of a society have the power to change the structures and institutions with which they lived or that people are agents of their own actions and behaviors. *Materialism theory* suggests that economic conditions are the determinant factors of cultural transformation. *Cultural patterns theory* emphasizes that different cultures have different principles that provide the framework for their unique values. This theory assumes that one can only understand a culture through its own values and perspectives. *Culture evolution theory* assumes that people, society, and culture change over time. Today, anthropology has become a discipline with several specializations, as Nader (2000, p. 609) noted "For most of the twentieth century, anthropology was marked by increased specialization." She emphasizes the new direction for anthropology in the twenty-first century as "an anthropology that is inclusive of all humankind, reconnecting the particular with the universal, the local and the global, nature and culture." She also stressed that culture must be viewed as "part of nature and the changing nature of nature is a subject for all of us" (p. 615).

Cross-Cultural Psychology

The fundamental focus of the field of cross-cultural psychology is the understanding of human diversity and how cultural factors or conditions affect human behavior (Berry, Poortinga, & Pandey, 1997). Similarly, Triandis (2000) suggested that "one of the purposes of cross-cultural psychology is to establish the generality of psychological findings" and that "the theoretical framework is universalistic, and assumes the psychic unity of humankind" (Kazdin, 2000, p. 361). A more comprehensive definition of cross-cultural psychology is offered by Berry and associates as "the study of similarities and differences in individual psychological functioning in various cultural and ethnic groups; of the relationships between psychological variables and sociocultural, ecological, and biological variables; and of current changes in these variables" (Berry, Poortinga, Segall, & Dasen, 1992, p. 2). Cross-cultural psychology can be viewed as "the systematic study of behavior and experience as it occurs in different cultures, is influenced by culture, or results in changes in existing culture" (Berry & Triandis, 2004, p. 527). Cross-cultural psychology has at least two traditions involving quantitative methods that rely on statistical comparisons across different cultures and qualitative methods that employ field study methods used by cultural anthropologists (*see* Berry & Triandis, 2004). Cross-cultural psychology is also defined as the study of overt (behavioral) and covert (cognitive, affective) differences between different cultures (Corsini, 1999, p. 238). Therefore, cross-cultural psychological research generally encompasses systematic analysis, description, and comparisons of various cultural groups or societies to develop general principles that may account for their similarities and differences (Corsini, 1999, p. 238).

Cross-cultural psychology has paid close attention to emic and etic approaches in psychological inquiry. An *emic approach* emphasizes the variations within cultural phenomena, whereas an *etic approach* focuses on differences across cultural groups. The emic approach is concerned with the unique issues and problems that are specifically found within one culture or group. More specifically, an emic approach studies behaviors, attitudes, and social values inside a culture using instruments developed within it. On the other hand, the etic approach studies behaviors, attitudes, and social values based on the assumption that they are universal and can employ instruments developed outside of a target population or society (Berry, 1969). However, both approaches suffer from conceptual and methodological dilemma. A purely emic approach can hinder true cross-cultural comparisons, and a purely etic approach may not actually reveal true cultural differences because it can impose external concepts and measures on unique culture or society. Malpass (1977, p. 1069) articulated the purpose of cross-cultural psychology as "a methodological strategy and a means of bringing into focus methodological and conceptual issues that are frequently encountered in unicultural research." Consequently, the development of sound measurement instruments that can capture true cultural differences and articulate cultural uniqueness are the fundamental challenges of cross-cultural psychology research.

Cross-Cultural Political Science Research

The foundation of political science is built on some fundamental theories such as freedom, democracy, and political equality, and political research focuses on the causal relationships of these theoretical variables (King, Murray, Salomon, & Tandon, 2004). There have been conflicting views of culture within the field of political science concerning the relevance of culture in political inquiry. Some view culture as having no function in the understanding of politics; others see it as the possible causes of political outcomes, such as the development and transformation of democracy across societies (Wedeen, 2002). Cross-cultural political scientists studied cultural changes and its consequences on social and political structures. Political scientists found strong relationships between the values and beliefs of mass publics and the existence of democratic institutions. These researchers identified 12 areas of human values and beliefs that can be found in different cultures of the world: ecology, economy, education, family, gender and sexuality, government and politics, health, individual, leisure and friends, morality, religion, society and nation, and work. Cultural changes that occur as a result of economic development are best understood as an interaction between economic development and the cultural heritage of a society. That is, each society's unique culture can mitigate or ignite the cultural changes that accompany economic development (Inglehart, Basanez, & Moreno 1998; Inglehart, 1999, 2000). Studies of political cultures are important to understand ethnic politics and the transformation of democracy (Pye, 1997). The well-being of individuals and societies are no doubt the product of different political systems. Indeed, political systems and structures can either foster or hinder the development of economic well-being and the protection of human rights.

Comparative Sociology

European fathers of sociology such as Durkheim and Weber believed that general social laws can be derived from the observed similarities among societies. On the other hand, observed differences among societies provide the understanding of social changes in different areas of the world (Steinhoff, 2001). Functionalism and modernization theories have served as two key theoretical frameworks for cross-cultural sociology. The functionalists view society as a combination of different components, and the society can only function smoothly if different internal components can work together. The modernists see social changes as the consequences of the transition from traditional values to modern (Steinhoof, 2001). Although sociologists often argue that all sociological research involves comparison (Grimshaw, 1973), comparative sociology is a recognized as "a method that is deemed to be quite different from other sociological methods of inquiry. When the concept of comparative sociology is used, this phrase then refers to the method of comparing different societies, nation-states or culture in order to show whether and why they are similar or different in certain respects" (Arts & Halman, 1999, p. 1). Kohn (1987, p. 714) attempted to categorize comparative sociology into four types: "Those in which nation is object of study; those in which nation is context of study; those in which nation is unit of analysis; and those that are transnational in character." Kohn emphasized the importance of cross-national research that views nation as context of study. This type of cross-national research focuses on: "Testing the generality of findings and interpretations about how certain social institutions impinge on personality" (p. 714). Kohn also noted that the term cross-national research is more straightforward than cross-cultural research because cross-cultural research can involve comparisons of different subgroups within a nation. Thus, sociological research involving nations can be referred to as cross-national research, and those involving subcultures within a nation are cross-cultural research.

Cross-cultural researchers from these disciplines have employed similar methodologies for data collection and analysis. The differences are their research orientation and interests. Cross-cultural psychology, with its emphasis on the effects of culture on social behavior and social cognition, provides social work with practical guides in designing social and psychological interventions that can confront both unique and common problems among individuals and groups. Cross-cultural–anthological research can enhance social work research because it provides social work researchers with both theoretical directions and methodological frameworks to understand how people from different cultures cope with their daily life situations. Cross-cultural political science research is useful to global social work practice and research. Understanding cultural factors in political developments is instrumental for social workers who are involved in global practices in various countries or governments. Although this book is not about global social work, globalization is the real process that is permeating every society and every culture (Tomlinson, 1999). How each society or political system reacts and accommodates globalization will impact the well-being of its citizens. Social work will have to determine how to confront the negative impacts of globalization on members of different societies. Comparative sociology research from both functionalism and modernization perspectives can be useful for cross-cultural research. For example, social work researchers can draw from these two major theoretical frameworks in their efforts to explain the breakdown of family systems as the breakdown in the communication of different family members or the ability of family members to move from traditional values to modern. The study of the causes of family dysfunction across societies is beneficial for social work in the development of culturally sensitive and appropriate family interventions.

The inquiry of the influences of culture on human behavior is also fundamental to social work as we attempt to devise and provide effective interventions to both individual and societal problems in different cultural contexts. The four dimensions of cultural values established by Hofstede (1980) and dimensions of personality established by McCrae and John (1992) could be useful for social work in developing cultural competence guidelines and training.

It is fair to say that cross-cultural social work research differs from other cross-cultural disciplines in its context and implications. Cross-cultural social work research can borrow both theories and methodologies from other disciplines and refine them to meet the new challenges of our profession in this global and diverse society.

Issues in Cross-Cultural Social Research and Evaluation

The common aim of cross-cultural or -national research in the social sciences is the systematic comparison of human behaviors, social values, and social structures and how these variables influence individuals or social systems between or among different cultural groups, including nations, societies, or subcultural groups within a larger national or social system.

Although the term "cross-cultural social work" was not indexed nor does it have a brief discussion as a major concept or issue in the last issue of the *Encyclopedia of Social Work*, the social work profession has a long history of recognizing the importance of cultural influences on human behaviors and social work practices. In the *Blackwell Encyclopedia of Social Work*, Robinson (2000, p. 222) suggests that "To meet the needs of culturally diverse populations, social workers must have an understanding of culturally consistent assessment, evaluation and treatment skills, as well as theoretical content." This prescription of multicultural social work appears to embrace the ideas of cross-cultural comparability of assessment, outcomes, treatment implementations, and causal explanations. The National Association of Social Workers (NASW) has its own standards for cultural competency (NASW, 2001). In its document, NASW endorses 10 cultural competence standards for its members encompassing ethics and values, self-awareness, cross-cultural knowledge, cross-cultural skills, service delivery, empowerment and advocacy, diverse workforce, professional education, language diversity, and cross-cultural leadership. Among these 10 standards, standard 4 describes cross-cultural skills with the following statement: "Social workers shall use appropriate methodological approaches, skills, and techniques that reflect the workers' understanding of the role of culture in the helping process." This standard is relevant and important to social work researchers and evaluators. This standard implies that social work researchers and evaluators should employ appropriate research instruments, methodologies, and statistical methods in conducting cross-cultural social work research and evaluation. The Council on Social Work Education (CSWE) also emphasizes the importance of cultural diversity in its educational policy and accreditation standards (CSWE, 2001). It requires that accredited social work programs must "educate students to recognize diversity within and between groups that may influence assessment, planning, intervention, and research. Students learn how to define, design, and implement strategies for effective practice with persons from diverse backgrounds" (CSWE, 2001, p. 9). Both NASW's standard of cultural competence and CSWE's educational policy and accreditation standards emphasize the importance of recognizing the cultural dimension of social work practice. This is also the foundation of cross-cultural social work research and evaluation.

The following are a few examples of common goals of cross-cultural social work research and evaluation:

1. To understand how people from different cultures cope with their life situations, including economic, physical, psychological, and social situations
2. To identify the risk factors of psychological and social pathology across cultures

3. To evaluate the appropriateness, effectiveness and impacts of social policies, programs, and interventions on the well-being of people from different cultures

From the intervention perspective, we can define cross-cultural social work as the implementation of evidence-based practices (interventions) across different cultural groups, communities, societies, and nations. Therefore, cross-cultural social work research and evaluation involves the study of the appropriateness and efficacy of evidence-based social work interventions across different cultural groups. The fundamental issue is whether a treatment or intervention is culturally appropriate and produces similar outcomes among clients of different cultures. We can also frame this issue as whether social workers can successfully implement a treatment or intervention proved to be effective for one cultural group for other groups that have different cultural backgrounds. The answer is contingent on several issues, but the most important is the cross-cultural equivalence of treatment and outcome measures. One cannot draw a valid conclusion about the efficacy of a treatment across different cultural populations if the treatment was operationalized and implemented in different manners for each cultural group. Furthermore, if the outcome measure bears no similarities in psychometric properties, then the comparison is not warranted.

Having a meaningful, appropriate, and practical research instrument or questionnaire is a prerequisite for the quality of cross-cultural social work research and evaluation. This allows social work researchers and evaluators to collect the correct data for either cross-cultural hypothesis testing or outcome evaluation.

There are two issues concerning measurements in cross-cultural social work research and evaluation: conceptual equivalence and statistical equivalence. Conceptual equivalence is the first step in designing and planning a cross-cultural research or evaluation project. This requires that key research variables and outcome measures must bear a conceptual equivalence across cultural groups of clients or participants. More specifically, both independent variables and dependent variables must bear similar meanings between two or among several comparative groups. Conceptual equivalence encompasses both linguistic equivalence and cultural equivalence. Linguistic equivalence refers to the equivalence of the translation of a concept or an instrument between the selected languages of clients or participants. Cultural equivalence requires that a research variable or treatment must be understood and accepted by clients/participants who come from different social structures with unique social orientations and value systems such as individualistic vs. collective social orientation.

Social work researchers and evaluators can achieve linguistic and cultural equivalence for the selected research variables or treatments via cultural translation and cultural evaluation of the content, format, and structure of the questionnaire items or research instruments. For example, when a question is developed to collect information on a symptom of depression, we need to ensure that such a symptom exists across cultural groups, that the language used in each cultural group reflects the meaning of such depressive symptom, and that the format of the question or item and the overall structure of the questionnaire are culturally relevant and appropriate for all cultural groups. Both linguistic and cultural equivalence may be achieved by employing appropriate cross-cultural translation procedures and expert evaluations.

How does a social work researcher know that a scale or an outcome measure has conceptual equivalence in two or more comparative cultural groups? The answer to this question relies on the information collected from both professionals and laypersons representing the cultural groups under investigation. This can be done through literature review, focus group meetings, town hall meetings, in-depth interviews with professionals and laypersons or prospective clients, and statistical analyses. When a scale is translated from one language to another, there are cross-cultural translation procedures that researchers and evaluators should follow. This book discusses and illustrates the use of both descriptive statistics and confirmatory factor analysis to evaluate cross-cultural equivalence of research instruments.

It should be noted that although this book emphasizes the importance of measurement equivalence in cross-cultural social work research and evaluation, the issues of cultural sensitivity and cultural appropriateness are the foundation of all types of social work research and interventions. Social work researchers may employ sound cross-cultural equivalent instruments in their research, but they will encounter resistance or non-cooperation from the target population if they are culturally insensitive and inappropriate in their relationship with the community. Similarly, evidence-based interventions must be implemented in different ethnic communities with cultural sensitivity and appropriateness.

The overall process of cross-cultural instrument development and assessment will be discussed in the following Chapter 2. The process can be applied at local (national) and international settings. Most of the practical issues are discussed from a national perspective. Researchers may have to modify some aspects of this process in global or international settings.

2

Process of Cross-Cultural Instrument Development and Assessment

*R*esearch instrument is defined as a systematic and standardized tool for data collection. It includes all types of research questionnaires and standardized scales. There are three methods of cross-cultural research instrument development: adopting an existing instrument, adapting or modifying an existing instrument, and developing a new instrument. To develop a cross-culturally valid questionnaire or instrument, the concepts or constructs selected for the investigation must be clearly defined and bear the same meanings across the selected cultural groups. No good questionnaire can be developed without clear definitions. This is a matter of utmost importance for all levels of cultural comparative research and evaluation, whether it is a gender or racial/ethnic comparison within one society or across nations. As Smith (2004) noted, "An essential goal of cross-national survey research is to construct questionnaires that are functionally equivalent across populations" (p. 3).

Adoption of existing instruments uses direct translation of the research instrument or questionnaire from the source language to the target language without considering cultural differences. This is an efficient and cost-effective method but suffers from potential problems of cultural inequivalence because researchers often pay too much attention to the linguistic equivalence and ignore the culturally conceptual equivalence. The problem with measurement adoption approach is the assumption of cultural equivalence between the source language and the target language. The researchers impose their cultural values or biases on the target population by assuming that the instruments they adopt carry the same meanings between their culture and the target culture.

Adaptation of an existing instrument calls for carefully translation and modification to achieve cultural equivalence between the source language and the target language (Pan & Puente, 2005). This approach requires the researchers or the research team to be competent in both cultures. There are different levels of adaptation, including the elimination of a part of the original instrument, replacing some items of the original scale with new items, or the application of the multilevel-translation procedure that avoids verbatim translation and thus emphasizes the equivalence of concepts not the equivalence of language between cultures.

Development a new instrument is a complicated task. Researchers have to start from a vague idea and go through numerous iterations of identifying and defining the research concepts and variables, transforming concepts to variables, and developing questions or items to capture the meanings of the research variables across different research populations.

The flowchart in Figure 2.1 outlines a process of cross-cultural instrument development. This flowchart suggests that the steps or phases of the process should be viewed as a self-reflective process in that one must always evaluate the current phase and go back to the previous phases for revision or modification until the final instrument can be accepted by all members of the research team. The first four steps of the process are similar for the efforts of developing a new instrument and adopting or adapting an existing instrument. The process of Cross-Cultural Questionnaire Development illustrated in the following flowchart will be developed throughout the book.

The flowchart in Figure 2.1 delineates the necessary steps in the process of cross-cultural instrument development. It begins with the preliminary tasks, including formulating the research aims from the context

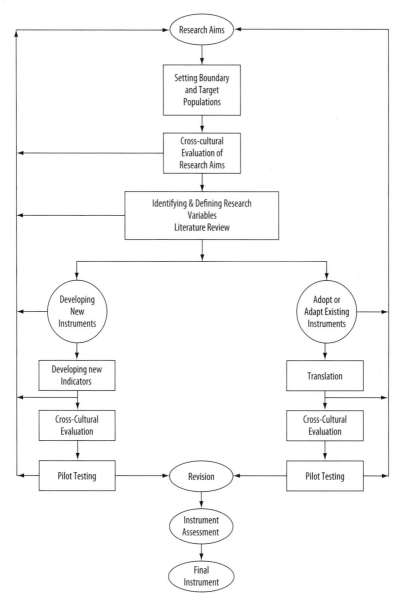

Figure 2.1 The Process of Cross-Cultural Instrument Development

of cross-cultural settings. The sources and motivation of research aims are generally as follows:

1. **Funding agencies or institutions.** Researchers are expected to develop the research aims that reflect the interests of a funding agency or institution. In this situation, researchers often do not have the flexibilities to do what they want to do.
2. **Community or national needs.** The researchers have to develop research aims that address the needs of communities or nations.
3. **Individual and team interests.** Researchers are free to do what interests them with less external constraints.

Once the research aims, questions, or hypotheses are identified, formulated, and agreed upon by key research personnel, the boundary and cross-cultural comparisons and the target populations must be thoroughly discussed. Some of the keys issues of this task are:

1. **Research locations.** Choosing the geographical areas to conduct the research project depends on the available resources, the representative of the locations, and the availability of and accessibility to the research participants.
2. **Number of comparison groups and sample sizes.** The research team must agree on the number of comparison groups and the number of participants representing each comparison group.
3. **Key characteristics of participants.** It is also important to decide on selection criteria, such as age, sex, education, incomes, and nature of social or psychological illness.

Representatives from the selected target populations, communities, or groups must be included in the evaluation of the research aims, questions, and hypotheses before others research tasks can be developed and implemented. The selected research aims must have similar levels of importance and meaningfulness among the participating cultural groups or populations.

The keys research variables are derived from the research aims, questions, and hypotheses. The task of identifying and defining the selected research variables is equally important as identifying and formulating the cross-cultural research aims. The variables must reflect the aims from a cross-cultural perspective.

After the variables are identified and defined, researchers can adopt or adapt existing instruments or develop new ones. The conducting of a comprehensive and systematic literature review can help researchers find existing instruments for their research aims. If there is a need to develop new instruments, then researchers should involve both experts and prospective participants in their attempts to define and measure the research variables. Adopting and adapting existing instruments requires the application of multilevel translation procedure to successfully translate the existing instruments from a source language to the target languages. Developing new instruments that can be used across different cultural or linguistic groups is complicated and expensive. In either case, systematic assessments of conceptual equivalence and measurement equivalence are required before the implementation of data collection and analysis.

The process illustrated in the flowchart suggests two general levels of analysis: qualitative and quantitative.

The qualitative level involves:

1. **Formulating the common research aims.** Researchers can use experts, in-depth interviews, and focus groups during the process of formulating the cross-cultural research aims for their projects.
2. **Setting the research boundaries and populations.** It is important for the researchers to have current demographic information of the prospective research populations. The use of the most recent census data is necessary for this task.
3. **Generating common hypotheses and variables across cultural groups.** The involvement of experts, community leaders, practitioners, and prospective research subjects through in-depth interviews and focus groups is needed. Social work researchers must be mindful of the potential benefits and risks to the community and clients caused by the outcomes of their hypothesis testing.
4. **Building the research team and support staff.** The research team and support staff must be both methodologically and culturally competent. All team members must be familiar with the cultures of the research populations. If possible, research team and support staff should also be members of the research groups, communities, or societies.

5. Establishing rapport with the communities and prospective participants. Well-designed research methods and instruments are necessary but not sufficient for the success of the research project. The researchers cannot implement their projects without the participation of the research populations. Establishing rapport with community leaders and providing relevant information about the projects to the communities are essential. The research team may develop a special Web site about the project and invite the community to engage in the research projects via the Web site.

The above tasks require in-depth discussion, exchange of ideas, and negotiations among all key stakeholders. It is always challenging to find consensus among a diverse group of stakeholders.

The quantitative level involves:

1. The collection of data
2. Assessing cross-cultural validity and reliability of the instruments

Careful preparation and planning for data collection is crucial for the success of data analyses. Assessing cross-cultural validity and reliability involves the establishment of cross-cultural psychometric equivalence or the similarities in the reliability and factorial structures of the measurement of key variables across cultural groups. Using the internal consistency coefficient and the correlation of an item with the overall scale is one way to check for statistical equivalence of a composite scale or index across cultural target groups (Van de Vijver & Leung, 1997). If a scale has five items, then the correlation of each item with the overall scale should be similar across the comparative groups. When a scale has a similar α-coefficient and correlation of item and overall scale, it is considered as having one of the indicators of statistical equivalence. Subsequently, social work researchers and evaluators can employ explanatory and confirmatory factor analyses to evaluate the factorial equivalence of a scale or an index across selected cultural groups. However, this does not warrant cross-cultural equivalence. One needs to look further into the factorial equivalence of such a scale. For a scale to be considered as having conceptual and statistical equivalence between two cultural groups under the investigation, its items (designed to capture the selected behavior, attitude, or psycho-social problem) must bear similar meanings in both cultural groups and should exhibit similar statistical evidence in terms of reliability and factorial structures.

The results of descriptive reliability analysis, factor analysis, and multisample confirmatory factor analyses will help the researchers to decide whether an instrument can be used across different research populations. This book will illustrate the application of SPSS and LISREL for the assessments of cross-cultural equivalence of the research instruments.

Chapter 3 covers the preliminary steps in the cross-cultural instrument development and assessments. These steps involve the recruitment and training of the support staff and prospective participants.

3

Preliminary Steps in Cross-Cultural Instrument Development

No matter how well a research project is prepared, there are always unforeseen circumstances, matters, and problems that force the researchers to confront and find resolutions. This chapter offers the readers some practical recommendations for the preparation of the preliminary steps in the process of cross-cultural research instrument development.

Research Aims

Cross-cultural research is expensive and time-consuming. A cross-cultural research project without meaningful and clear research aims would only lead to confusion. Funding sources often determine the scope and aims of a cross-cultural research project. In this situation, the researchers respond to specific instructions of the funding institution and the research aims must articulate the vision and goals of the funding institution. Regardless of funding sources, cross-cultural social work researchers should always involve different stakeholders (e.g., clients, service providers, community leaders) in defining and formulating the research aims. The researchers should be aware that their research aims must bear similar meanings across cultural groups and the expected outcomes will improve or enhance the well-being of the target populations, such as health, mental health, quality of life, or living standards.

Setting Boundary and Target Populations

Cross-cultural research involves systematic comparisons of selected variables between two or among more cultural groups. The researchers need to identify the key variables for the comparisons, Among groups which they will make such comparisons. Obviously, the boundary of a cross-cultural research project is defined by the available resources, the feasibility of the project, and the participation of the target populations. The research team should seek community support from various cultural groups at local levels. If the research involves cross-national comparisons, then seeking support from governments, institutions, and political leaders becomes even more crucial for the success of the project.

Cross-Cultural Evaluations of Research Aims

Once the preliminary research aims, variables, and target populations are identified, the research team should call for at least one focus group of stakeholders to evaluate the importance and relevancy of the research aims. With current Internet technology, the research team can create a Web site with a "chat room" that allows team members and designated consultants or prospective participants to engage in the group evaluation of the research aims. The "chat room" approach is less expensive and more convenient for participants. Researchers can also participate in a "video" calling conference from their own PC or laptop with Webcam and a headset. There are three basic questions that require clear answers before the research project can move to the next phases:

1. Are the proposed research aims meaningful among the cultural groups?
2. Do the proposed aims have cross-cultural equivalence among the cultural groups?

3. Will the potential results have any meaningful impacts on the quality of the life of the comparative populations?

If these questions are not satisfactorily answered, then the research team should revise the research aims until they are acceptable.

Identifying and Defining Variables and Literature Review

Once the research aims are evaluated by the research team and stakeholders, the research team must identify and define the relevant variables that reflect the research aims. The variables must bear similar meanings across the selected comparative groups. Although Internet "chat room" and video calling conferences over the Internet can be useful, the dynamic of face to face interaction among the research team members is important for the process of identifying and defining the research variables. It is suggested that a focus group involving the research team and stakeholder is necessary to generate meaningful variables for the project. The goals of the focus group should include:

1. Developing a comprehensive list of variables representing the research aims.
2. Select the variables that appear to bear some levels of cultural equivalence among the comparative groups.
3. Define the selected variables that capture cultural differences both within and between groups.

Once the variables are selected and defined, the researchers should review the existing literature for the operationalization of the variables—that is, to identify any existing instruments that can be used to measure the selected variables. If the team members and the expert consultants agree that an existing instrument is adequate and appropriate for the project, the next step is to translate the instrument into the target languages. The translation will be subjected to in-depth evaluation and pilot testing before it can be used. Chapter 4 is devoted to the procedure of cross-cultural translation. If there are no existing instruments, the research team needs to develop a valid and reliable instrument that can be used across the selected cultural groups.

Cross-Cultural Research Support Team

Building a strong research support team is one of the most crucial tasks to secure the successful implementation of the research projects. The support team includes cultural experts, community advisors, interviewers for cognitive interviews, moderators for focus groups, and translators for the translation process.

Cultural Expert Recruitment Criteria

The research team will have to rely on cultural experts to assist the process of instrument development from the evaluation of the existing instruments to the construction of new instruments. The following criteria can be used as a guide to select cultural experts to participate in the development and evaluation of indicators.

Language Proficiency

It is difficult for a researcher who has no or limited language skills to conduct a research project on an ethnic or cultural group whose language is different from the researcher's language. In such a situation, the researcher should bring to the team individuals who have the language skills to serve as cultural expert for the research project.

Relevant Professional Credential

A good cultural expert must have appropriate training in the field related to the problem under investigation. Having language skills of a cultural group is necessary for a cultural expert but this is not sufficient. This expert must also be trained in the field. A cultural expert who is fluent in the language of the research population and highly educated but who lacks a formal training related to the research project would not be able to help the research team to evaluate the research instrument effectively. When it is difficult to find ideal cultural experts, the researcher should offer adequate training to the prospective experts before allowing them to engage in the instrument development and evaluation process.

Knowledge of History, Geography, Arts, Literature, and Customs

The cultural expert should have some knowledge of history, geography, arts, literature, and customs of a research population. This background gives the expert insights into the understanding of how members of that group behave. The cultural expert who possesses these qualities will better help the research team throughout the process of instrument development.

Bilingual and Bicultural Ability

When the researchers borrow a research concept that has been well-defined in one language (e.g., English), it is useful to have cultural experts who are bilingual and bicultural to help the research team with the translation of the selected concept to the target language.

Interviewer Recruitment Criteria

Interviewers will be needed to conduct both cognitive interviews and pilot survey interviews. The interviewers should have the following characteristics:

1. Knowledge of the culture of the target research group or population
2. A sense of respect and tolerance for cultural differences
3. Ability to communicate with interviewees
4. Flexibility to adapt to interviewees' situations

Participant Recruitment Criteria

Participants from different target populations will be needed to participate in cognitive interviews, focus groups, and pilot surveys. They should be selected based on the following criteria.

Having an ability to communicate openly

Selected participants should have an ability to speak for themselves and on behalf of others. Because the researchers want to learn how members of a cultural or ethnic group communicate their feelings and attitudes toward a particular social or psychological phenomenon, it is important to recruit prospective participants who can help the researcher to define such a phenomenon in a common language that can be understood by other group members. Participants' observations of friends and relatives can also give the researcher valuable insight into the concept of interest.

Having previous experience relevant to the research concepts or problems

If the researchers want to develop a measure of coping with disasters, then only those prospective participants who have had direct or indirect experiences with disasters should be invited to participate in in-depth interviews.

Having the will to share experiences with others

Participants who are willing to discuss their feelings or experiences with others will help the researchers to collect relevant information in defining and articulating the research concept.

Focus Group Moderator Recruitment Criteria

The quality of the data collected from the focus groups also depend on the quality of the focus group moderator. An effective focus moderator should have the following qualifications.

Cultural Competency

The moderator has to have an in-depth-knowledge of the culture of the target population to appreciate the nuances of behaviors and attitudes of the participants from their own cultural meanings and context. This will help generate participants' engagement in the group discussion.

Language Competency

The moderator is expected to be fluent in at least two languages to fully facilitate the focus group in the evaluation of linguistic and cultural comparability of the research instrument.

Creativity

The moderator has to be able to think on his/her feet and be able to create group dynamics that generate meaningful discussion and evaluation of the research instrument.

Analytical Skills

Good analytical skills help the moderator to raise meaningful questions and guide participants to the right discussion.

Verbal skills

The moderator should be able to communicate and articulate the research aims as well as the meanings of the research variables and instruments to the participants. The moderator's verbal skills will stimulate participants to stay focused on their tasks during the focus group meetings.

Detail-Oriented

The moderator should be able to see through the details of the instruments, research procedures, and goals and objectives of the research instruments. This ability will help the moderators to stay on course and probe for subtle information from the participants.

Listening Skills

The success of a focus group largely depends on the ability of the moderator to listen to the participants. Listening and showing respect to participants' ideas will help them to reveal the information they would not reveal if they thought the moderator was not interested in them.

Empathy

Being able to share participants' feelings and appreciate their attitudes in a group setting will attract more attention from participants and their willingness to share their views and thoughts concerning the purpose of the focus group meeting.

Community Advisor Recruitment Criteria

Having knowledgeable and committed committee advisors will strengthen the research project. Following is a list of people that the researchers may want to invite them to serve as advisors for a cross-cultural research project.

Prospective Consumers Research

Professionals who will use the results of the research to improve their practices and interventions that will affect the life of their clients.

Prospective Participants or Subjects

Individuals who are members of the research population from which the research will be conducted. These are the people who will be directly affected by the outcomes of the research.

Community or Civic Leaders

Individuals who hold notable community leadership positions in the community such as religious leaders, educators, politicians, and leaders of various social organizations in the community from which the research will be conducted.

Trained Professionals in the Field of Interest

Researchers who have conducted research that is similar to the current projects or who have special training in the areas related to the current research project.

This chapter has provided a list of essential tasks and recommendations for the researchers to prepare before engaging in the construction and assessment of cross-cultural research instruments. Without clear and meaningful research aims, it is difficult for the researchers to move ahead with the project. Similarly, without a strong research support staff and the right participants, the research team will not be able to successfully develop meaningful research instruments.

Chapter 4 is about the translation of existing research instruments from a source language to different target languages. The potential threats of research instrument translation are numerous, including both technical and conceptual aspects. The readers will find hands-on experiences and practical guides to carry out the translation of a research instrument successfully.

4

Adopting or Adapting Existing Instruments

Cross-Cultural Translation and Related Issues

Both adopting and adapting existing research instruments often require the translation of the selected instrument from a source language to a target language. Cross-cultural translation is one of the major tasks in cross-cultural research. The task of translation becomes more challenging when an instrument is translated into two or more target languages simultaneously.

This chapter will *(1)* review existing cross-cultural translation approaches and offer the reader with practical guidelines; *(2)* present a multilevel translation process encompassing back translation, expert evaluation, cognitive interviews, focus group evaluation, and field evaluation; and *(3)* offer a guide for best practices in selecting translators to perform cross-cultural translation. Several examples will be presented to illustrate potential biases in cross-cultural translation and cross-cultural data analysis.

Researchers have employed a variety of translation approaches, and it appears that no single approach has become universal. In cross-cultural psychology, Brislin, Lonner, and Thorndike (1973) recommended that cross-cultural translation should involve back-translation, bilingual techniques, committee approach, and pretest. More specifically, back-translation is a process wherein an instrument is translated from its original language to a different language, and the translated version of the instrument is translated back to the original language to assure conceptual equivalence.

Maneesriwongul and Dixon (2004) reviewed 47 studies that involved cross-cultural translation and concluded that there is a lack of consensus on the standards of cross-cultural translation. There are three common approaches of cross-cultural translation that have been used: *(1)* forward-only translation approach is a one-way translation from the source language to a target language. This approach is not recommended because of the lack of reliability and validity evaluation; *(2)* forward translation with testing approach is stronger, but it also does not address the issue of cross-cultural validity and reliability; and *(3)* back translation approach appears to be stronger than the previous two approaches, but it tends to emphasize the literal translation or linguistic equivalence, which does not warrant cross-cultural equivalence.

Harkness (2003) has offered a more desirable approach of survey questionnaire translation process called Translation, Review, Adjudication, Pre-testing and Documentation (TRAPD). This approach is a committee-based approach that involves translators, reviewers, and adjudicator. Committee or team approaches of translation have been recognized as a more effective approach compared with other approaches (Guillemin, Bombardier, & Beaton, 1993; Harkness, Pennell & Schoua-Glusber, 2004). The translation can be performed via parallel translations or split translations. In parallel translations, translators work independently before submitting their translation for committee review and evaluation. When two or more nations and groups share the same language, each group can translate a part of the whole research instrument (i.e., split translation). The committee approach and TRADP process do not address the issue of gender representatives in either translation or evaluation. In this book, gender representative is required in questionnaire construction and translation process. Harkness (2003) has suggested that translators are "skilled practitioners who have received training on translating questionnaires," (p. 36). Skilled translators should have adequate knowledge on the research topic and population to perform valid translation. It would be difficult for a translator who has his/her formal training in engineering to perform a translation of a research questionnaire for a study of depression. This should also be applied to the reviewers of the translation of the questionnaire and those who adjudicate the final translation of the questionnaire. Harness (2003) recommends the use of "team approaches" for cross-cultural translation of research instruments. The key advantage of this approach is that team members whose diverse backgrounds will help the team to determine the best translation outcomes (Guillemin, Bombardier, & Beaton, 1993).

Figure 4.1 illustrates the cross-cultural translation process from the source language (e.g., English) to the target language (e.g., Vietnamese). Because there is no gold standard for cross-cultural translation procedure, this book combines the previously used cross-cultural translation procedures into the following schematic description. This translation process is time-consuming and requires the researchers to carefully select

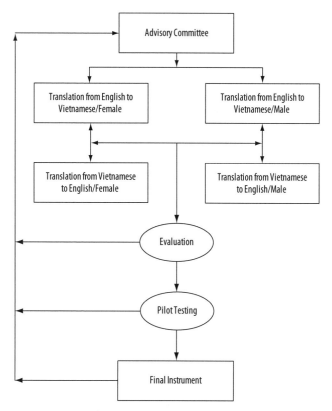

Figure 4.1 Cross-Cultural Translation Process

advisory committees and translators and to use different methods of translation evaluation to achieve quality cross-cultural translation of an instrument.

The five-step flowchart depicted in Figure 4.1 illustrates a comprehensive procedure for cross-cultural translation involving one target group.

Advisory Committee

The first step in the cross-cultural translation procedure is to form an advisory committee that will work with the research team to select an appropriate instrument or a survey questionnaire that can be used to collect data for the research project. This advisory committee should be comprised of professionals who are trained in the area of the research interest and who understand the nature and scope of the research problems or questions concerning the research population. The rationale for these selection criteria is straightforward—only individuals who are trained in the area of research interest can help the research team to select the appropriate instruments or measures for the research purposes. These individuals also need to be culturally and linguistically competent. If the research project involves more than two groups, then each group should have at least one female and one male expert representative serving on the advisory committee. This gender representative principle should apply for all translation activities. More than one expert in each group is called for to assure the diversity of voice and perspectives. Throughout the book, the author emphasizes the representation of both genders in all key instrument development because gender is a complex variable encompassing sex, socialization, identity, and communication (Cameron, 1988).

Forward and Backward Translation

The second step is to recruit and hire competent bilingual translators. The research team should work with the advisory committee to screen, hire, and provide adequate training on key aspects of the research project to the selected translators. For each linguistic group, there should be at least four translators, two females and two males, who work independently to perform translation and back-translation from the source language (e.g., English) to the target language (e.g., Vietnamese) and vice versa. The translators must have adequate understanding of the research aims and key research concepts to perform a valid translation. Translators must be instructed to avoid verbatim translation but emphasize the comparability of the concepts and ideas between the source and target languages.

Evaluation

The third step is to evaluate the translation. The research team should employ multi-evaluation methods, including expert appraisal and review (evaluation committee), cognitive interviews, focus groups, and pilot testing. An independent group of experts or the same advisory committee should evaluate the translation and back-translation version of the translated instrument. This group should meet with the translators to clarify and verify their translations. The following evaluation matrix in Table 4.1 can be used for the expert group evaluation. The evaluation matrix allows the research team to collect both quantitative and qualitative evaluation information. Each evaluator is asked to respond "yes" or "no" to each evaluation criterion and to provide a brief explanation for the rating. Simultaneously, the team should conduct cognitive interviews and focus groups as the integral parts of the evaluation process.

Language Clarity

Committee members evaluate the use of words and syntax of the translated item and its back-translation.

Appropriateness

Committee members determine whether the translated items are culturally appropriate in both language and meaning for the target population.

Difficulty

Committee members determine whether the translated items are difficult for prospective respondents or participants to understand and to respond.

Table 4.1 Translation Evaluation Matrix

Evaluation	Member 1		Member 2		Member 3	
	Yes Explanation	No Explanation	Yes Explanation	No Explanation	Yes Explanation	No Explanation
Item 1						
Language Clarity						
Appropriateness						
Difficulty						
Relevance						
Item 2						
Language Clarity						
Appropriateness						
Difficulty						
Relevance						
Item 3						
Language Clarity						
Appropriateness						
Difficulty						
Relevance						
Item k						
Language Clarity						
Appropriateness						
Difficulty						
Relevance						

Relevance

Committee members determine whether the translated items are culturally relevant to the participants' experiences in real-life situations.

Cognitive Interviews

As mentioned earlier, cognitive interviews should be used to evaluate the research questionnaire (Rothgeb, Willis & Forsyth, 2005). The cognitive interview is a form of in-depth interview that allows the prospective research subjects to express their feelings toward the research instrument in terms of its appropriateness, usefulness, and meanings and to explain how they understand the questionnaire and how they respond to the questionnaire. The research team works with the evaluation committee to recruit a representative sample of at least 6 to 12 prospective research subjects for each target group to participate in the cognitive interviews. The sample of size recommended here is similar to the sample sizes recommended for other types of qualitative research (Morgan, 1988). Think-aloud and verbal probing approaches of cognitive interviewing should be used concurrently. The interviewers begin the interviews by reading the translated item to the participants and asking them to say whatever comes to their minds as they listen to the item. Subsequently, the interviewers should use the criteria in the evaluation matrix (*see* Table 4.1) to probe for more information. Digital recording should be used as the means of data collection.

Interviewers must be trained to have a clear understanding of the purpose of the research project, the meanings of the research questionnaire, and its items. Interviewers must possess skills to probe for in-depth answers and encourage the participants to reveal their thoughts and feelings concerning the translated items of the questionnaire. Interviewers should probe the participants regarding four aspects of the quality of the translation: language clarity, cultural appropriateness, difficulty, and relevance. Clarity refers to the use of words and syntax of the items. Appropriateness refers to the suitability of the translated items to the research participants' culture and values. Difficulty refers to the participants' cognitive ability to respond or react to each translated item. Relevance refers to the connection of the translated items to respondents' real-life experiences within their cultural context.

Focus Groups

Focus groups can be conducted simultaneously with cognitive interviews as a part of the evaluation process. The research team should conduct at least three focus groups: one female group, one male group, and one combined gender group. The single-sex group allows a more comfortable atmosphere for the participants to bring up issues that are sex-related before they can be discussed in both-gender groups. Each linguistic or cultural group should have a minimum of six participants (Fayers & Machin, 2007). Having within- and between-gender-group and culture-group meetings sounds complicated, but they are desirable because these meetings will generate rich information necessary for a comprehensive assessment of cross-cultural equivalence. Group members should receive the complete translation of the questionnaire at least 1 week prior to the focus group meeting. Focus group participants are asked to review and discuss the quality of the translation using the four quality criteria presented in Table 4.1. All members must have an equal opportunity to discuss their ideas concerning the translation. The moderator must ensure the participation of each member during the focus group meetings. Discussions should be audio- or video-recorded. Each meeting should be no more than 2 hours, because the participants will be more likely to lose focus and interest in longer meetings.

Data Analysis and Synthesis

Evaluation data compiled from committee evaluation, cognitive interviews, and focus groups are transcribed and edited for an overall evaluation. Translators, advisory committees, and the researchers will work together to revise and refine the research instrument or survey questionnaire for a field pilot testing.

Pilot Testing

The purpose of the pilot testing is to establish the feasibility of the research instrument, evaluate the quality of interviewing methods, and assess the sources of missing data and other aspects of the implementation of the research instrument. Structured pilot interviews via survey are conducted for reliability and validity evaluations. If possible, telephone interviews, face-to-face interviews, and mail surveys can be used simultaneously to improve the validity of the translation. A reliable and valid translated questionnaire should produce similar data regardless of the data collection methods. The sample size of the pilot survey test is determined by the size of the instruments and resources. From the factor analysis perspective, each item of a scale requires the minimum number of 5 to 10 subjects (Fayers & Machin, 2007). If the questionnaire consists of several standardized scales, then the team can use the scale with the largest number of items or questions as the guide to determine sample size. Random sampling is always a desirable method to draw a sample, but it is often not feasible. Therefore, the research team should make every effort to recruit individuals from diverse backgrounds of the target population to participate in the pilot test.

Finally, once data from the pilot tests are compiled and analyzed, the evaluation committee will review the results and work with the research team to finalize the translation. The research team will combine data collected from expert groups, cognitive interviews, focus groups, and pilot survey testing to finalize the research instrument for data collection. The process of translation is time-consuming and can be expensive. However, the benefits of having a valid and reliable translation outweigh the cost and time that the researchers have to spend to achieve the most desirable translated instrument. Researchers should continue to update and refine the translations of cross-cultural instruments to catch up with the changes of languages, culture, and communication.

Cross-Cultural Translation Issues and Biases

There are several issues and biases concerning cross-cultural translation, such as the quality of translated instruments and potential problems in using secondary data analysis for cross-cultural comparisons. These issues and biases often are the results of the attempts to replicate existing measurements that were developed in a source language such as English for studies among people whose primary languages are not English. Biases are also the results of pooling data from various sources for global comparisons. Some of the potential biases in cross-cultural translation and analysis can be avoided with careful planning and implementation of translation procedures and analysis.

Multilingual Translation

When two or more linguistic groups are involved in a comparative study, the cross-cultural translation process becomes more complicated. The procedure illustrated in Figure 4.1 must be modified to achieve optimum translation outcomes. The composition of the "Advisory Committee" and the "Evaluation Committee" must include individuals from all participating groups. Members of these committees should be able to communicate through a common language. For example, if a researcher plans to study depression among Vietnamese and Russian immigrants in the United States, then the evaluation committee members are expected to be bilingual (English–Vietnamese and English–Russian).

Recruit and Train Translators

In addition to language proficiency, prospective translators are expected to have knowledge of the research field and the culture of the target population. They should be trained to have a good understanding of the research aims and the meanings of the research variables. Translators must also have good communication and listening skills to work with other translators and the research team. When there are no available trained and experienced translators, the team must design a special training program to prospective translators. This training program should include cultural characteristics, linguistic requirements such as terminologies related to the research topics, and substantive knowledge of the research area.

Recruit Subjects for Evaluation

Prospective research subjects or participants from the comparative cultural groups or communities are recruited to participate in the evaluation process of the translation. These individuals need to have good language skills in their own language and critical thinking ability to evaluate the quality and accuracy of the translation. They are people who can represent their own ethnic or cultural groups. It is expected that these individuals have a good understanding of the research aims, the under-lying purposes of the research instruments, and an ability to speak for themselves and on behalf of their communities.

Recruit and Train Interviewers for Translation Evaluation

Interviewers are recruited and trained to conduct cognitive interviews for the evaluation of the translation. They must go through rigorous train-ing, including instruction on how to read the questionnaire clearly and probe for appropriate information, record and maintain quality data, and respect and protect participants' confidentiality.

Verbatim Translation

When a researcher uses an instrument developed in the language that is different from the language of the target population, verbatim translation of the selected research instrument is not recommended. Equivalence of language translation often confuses respondents from a different culture. For example, in the CESD scale, there is the item "I felt that I was just as good as other people." This item appears to be straightforward and should be easily translated to other languages, but it turns out that when it is translated into Russian and Vietnamese, the item has very poor reli-ability. Looking back on our translation process, we did not pay as much attention to this item as we did with other difficult item such as, "I felt that I could not shake off the blues even with help from my family or friends." The translation team gave more effort in translating this item than to the item "I felt that I was just as good as other people." To avoid verbatim translation of those items that appear to be straightforward, the translators should give equal attention to all items. In the case of the item "I felt that I could not shake of the blues even with help from my family or friends," two groups of translators (three females and three males) worked independently to translate the difficult items of the question-naire. The two groups met with the Principal Investigator (P.I.) to have an open discussion on the similarities and differences of the group trans-lation to arrive at a consensus. The group discussed meanings of the dif-ficult items in English and their translated meanings in Vietnamese. The final translated items did not have language equivalence but did have cul-tural and conceptual equivalence. Table 4.2 demonstrates the reliability

Table 4.2 Corrected Item–Total Correlation of "Shake off the Blues" and "As Good as other People"

	Vietnamese	Russian
Shake off the blues	0.634	0.675
As Good as Other People	**0.013**	**0.044**

of these two items in the Russian and Vietnamese sample. Differences in "Corrected Item–Total" correlation between different cultural groups is a sign of poor cross-cultural comparability (van de Vijver & Leung, 1997).

Single Translator

The use of a single translator is not recommended because of the lack of validity and reliability checks for the quality and accuracy of the translation (Maneesriwongul & Dixon, 2004). This bias becomes even more serious when the researcher has no language skills and is foreign to the target population.

Translators Without Appropriate Training Background

Translators who have no training background relevant to the research questions will not be able to perform valid and reliable translation of the research instrument. For example, a translator who is fluent in the language of the target research population, but who has no training in public health or social work, would not be able to produce a quality translation of the research instrument designed to collect data on health and mental health problems.

Failure to Evaluate the Validity and Reliability After Translation

One should never assume that if an instrument has been well-developed for one particular group, it is sufficient to translate it and replicate it in another group without a reaffirmation of its validity and reliability. It is recommended that researchers always evaluate the factor structure or configuration of the scale and its internal consistency once it is translated to the target language.

Inconsistency of Translation Procedure

When cross-cultural comparison is performed on a variable that has been translated from one original language to different target languages, one should be cognizant of the consistency of the translation procedures. Inconsistency of the translation procedures will impact the equivalence of reliability and validity of the measurement of the research variables, and the results could be severely biased. Table 4.3 illustrates the differences of internal consistency as the result of inconsistent translation procedures. Each of the studies presented in Table 4.3 employs different procedures of cross-cultural translation.

The statistics presented in Table 4.3 suggest that the three items of the CESD Scale have somewhat weak cross-cultural equivalence. The "depressed" item has cross-cultural equivalence between the Chinese and Russian samples. The "I felt lonely" item has a similar corrected item–total correlation between the Russian and Vietnamese samples. The "I felt sad" item also has a similar corrected item–total correlation between the Russian and Vietnamese samples. When we examined the equivalence of Cronbach's α-coefficients across the four samples, the only two samples that exhibited similar Cronbach's α-coefficients are the Chinese and the Japanese. Nevertheless, the corrected inter-item correlation of the "I felt Sad" item appears to be different between the two samples.

Different reliability statistics presented in Table 4.3 could be either cultural, methodological, or both. Cultural variations are more difficult to recognize than methodological variations. From the methodological perspective, these studies employed different translation procedures. The Japanese survey used "an extensive translation, back translation, retranslation, and pilot testing process in order to ensure a very high degree of comparability," (Sugisawa et al., 2002, p. 791; Lianget al., 2005).

Table 4.3 Corrected Item–Total Correlation of Three CESD Items

CESD Items	Chinese ($n = 175$)	Japanese ($n = 2119$)	Russian ($n = 299$)	Vietnamese ($n = 339$)
I felt depressed	0.587	**0.483**	0.591	**0.790**
I felt lonely	**0.472**	0.565	0.637	0.674
I felt sad	**0.507**	0.524	0.712	0.710
Cronbach's α	**0.697**	0.705	0.798	**0.853**

The Russian and Chinese surveys used one professional bilingual translator, committee evaluation, and pilot testing to ensure comparability (Tran, Aroian, Balsam & Conway, 2000; Wu, Tran & Amjad, 2004). Overall, the translation procedure of the Japanese survey was more desirable than the Russian and Chinese surveys. The Vietnamese studies used a similar approach of translation as the Japanese survey; however, it emphasized the use of equal numbers of female and male translators to avoid gender biases in translation (Tran, Ngo & Conway, 2003). These statistics suggest that one should be cautious in using the composite scores of these items for the purpose of cross-cultural comparisons, especially when one compares the meaning of these items across groups.

Inconsistency in Research Designs and Data Collection

When pooling data from different studies for statistical comparisons, researchers must account for the variations of designs and data collection methods. The results in Table 4.3 also suggest that the variation of study designs can affect the reliability and validity of the research instrument.

Cultural Variation Within the Same Linguistic Population

Researchers could be mistaken in assuming that language is the only marker of cultural similarities or differences. Sharing the same language does not warrant an equivalence of measurement. Table 4.4 presents the corrected item–total correlation of the five items that were designed to measure "negative" feelings or negative well-being among three groups of Hispanic elderly individuals (Davis, 1997). Although the respondents are members of three ethnic groups that share similar languages (Spanish and English), the statistics presented in Table 4.4 suggest that the selected items of negative well-being exhibit variation in reliability.

The statistics presented in Table 4.4 indicate that there is a variation of reliability of the items across the three ethnic groups that share similar languages. These three major groups of Hispanics do not share the same culture. They have different immigration histories and are very diverse in terms of family values, religion, and socio-economic backgrounds (Bean & Gillian, 2003; U.S. Census Bureau, 2001). This suggests that researchers should not assume that similarity of languages is equivalent to similarity of measurement. It is always a good practice to verify

Table 4.4 Corrected Item–Total Correlation of Five Bradburn's Negative Items

Negative Items	Survey (n = 2235)	Cuban (n = 692)	Mexican (n = 757)	Puerto Rican (n = 358)
Restless	0.480	0.432	0.459	**0.570**
Lonely	0.526	**0.451**	0.540	0.528
Bored	0.532	**0.430**	0.523	0.598
Depressed	0.574	0.536	0.566	**0.648**
Upset	0.294	0.243	0.292	0.261
Cronbach's α	0.722	0.665	0.718	0.755

the equivalence of the measurement of the variables used among the comparative groups, even if they share a language.

Different Language of Interview Within a Cultural Group

Language of interview can influence the reliability of an instrument even if it is used within the same cultural group. Respondents of The National Survey of Hispanic Elderly could be interviewed in English or in Spanish. A small number of respondents chose to be interviewed in English ($n = 308$), and the majority were interviewed in Spanish. It should be noted that the survey instrument was developed in English and translated into Spanish. Table 4.5 contains the reliability analysis of five negative item scales.

Although three of five items appeared to have similar corrected item–total correlation, the item "Restless" had a poorer correlation in the sample of English interviews, whereas the item "Upset" had a poorer

Table 4.5 Corrected Item–Total Correlation of Five Bradburn's' Negative Items between English and Spanish

Negative Items	English Interviews (n = 308)	Spanish Interviews (n = 1991)
Restless	**0.369**	0.496
Lonely	0.580	0.518
Bored	0.524	0.533
Depressed	0.523	0.581
Upset	0.370	**0.284**
Cronbach's α	0.722	0.724

corrected item–total correlation in the sample of Spanish interviews. Researchers can control for this problem by making sure that interviewers in different languages follow the same protocols. Languages of interview can be considered as a covariate in multivariable analysis, such as multiple regression analysis or other multivariate statistical procedures.

This chapter provides an overview of existing translation procedures and illustrates a multilevel translation process and procedure. The author used existing cross-cultural data to demonstrate potential biases of cross-cultural translation. The quality of the translation of adopted or adapted instruments is determined by its reliability and validity. The researchers can use the pilot evaluation data to decide whether an instrument is ready to be implemented. The techniques to assess the cross-cultural reliability and validity of the research instruments will be explained and illustrated in Chapters 6 and 7. Chapter 5 is devoted to the process of developing and constructing new cross-cultural research instruments.

5

Developing New Instruments

Developing new cross-cultural research instruments is an enormous task, and it requires careful consideration from the researchers to ensure that the instruments measure what they are designed to measure and can also capture cultural differences and similarities among the comparative groups. It is always challenging to develop an "etic" instrument that captures the shared meanings among the comparative cultural groups and an "emic" instrument that can measure the unique aspects of each cultural group (Smith, 2004). Developing and constructing cross-cultural research instruments must be a collaborative endeavor of the research team and the stakeholders. Inputs from cultural experts, prospective research respondents or clients, and service providers should be an integral part of every step or phase in cross-cultural measurement development and construction.

This chapter focuses on the foundation of measurement and the process of cross-cultural instrument development. The foundation of measurement involves some fundamental elements such as *concept, indicators, latent variables, reflective* or *effect indicators, causal* or *formative indicators*, and *theoretical framework*. These terms will be illustrated by examples relevant to social work. Once the research concepts and indicators are identified and defined, researchers need to transform them into a research instrument such as a survey questionnaire or a standardized scale. In cross-cultural research or evaluation, the selected concepts, indicators, and latent variables must be culturally relevant and appropriate among the target populations or communities.

Foundation of Measurement

The goal of a scientific social work theory is to explain the relationships among phenomena or constructs according to a set of facts, propositions, or principles. There are two aspects of a theory—one explains the relationships between theoretical constructs, such as self-esteem and depression; the other explains the relationship between a construct and its measures, such as depression and the items of a scale that were developed to measure depression. Researchers have no basis to explain the relationships between self-esteem and depression if these variables are not defined and measured. However, self-esteem and depression are psychological status that cannot be observed and measured directly as incomes, education, or age. Researchers have to identify observable and measurable indicators to capture the dimensions and levels of self-esteem and depression before they can test or evaluate their relationships statistically. In measurement development, researchers focus on the relationships between the constructs and their respective observable indicators (Edwards & Bagozzi, 2000).

The goal of scientific social work inquiry is to investigate the relationships among variables—that is, whether they are correlational or causal. Many human behaviors, attitudes, social, psychological conditions, or phenomena cannot be observed directly. Therefore, researchers have to construct measures to quantify the abstract concepts of interest, such as client satisfaction or motivation. Bollen (1989) stated, "Measurement is the process by which a concept is linked to one or more latent variables, and these are linked to observed variables" (p. 180). For example, client satisfaction is an abstract concept or a psychological reaction to external observable conditions or situations (e.g., interventions, services), and to ascertain whether the clients are satisfied or how much they are satisfied with the services or interventions they received from social workers or social service agencies, there must be a systematic way to determine such abstract psychological reaction. Researchers have to develop measurable instruments that carry some numeral values, hierarchical order, or categories that indicate whether clients are satisfied or not (dichotomous measure); whether their satisfaction is at low or high levels on an ordinal scale from low to high; or whether their satisfaction can be determined on a scale from 0 to 20 (interval or ratio). Whatever levels of measurement we use, we need to have a way to observe and record client satisfaction from the clients. In the social sciences literature, the abstract variables or concepts are called *latent variables*. We can only measure the latent variables through their observable indicators. In this case, researchers can measure the latent variable of client satisfaction by a set of questions (i.e., observable indicators) designed to capture all possible aspects and levels of client satisfaction. This is the process of developing observed indicators and linking these indicators to their respective latent variables.

Defining and Measuring Concepts

If social work researchers want to measure client satisfaction in a social service agency, then the most feasible and practical way to assess this construct is to ask the clients directly. The researcher needs to define client satisfaction in a clear and concise term. For example, client satisfaction can be defined as the extent to which the services meet the clients' needs and perception of the quality of the services. As the result, this construct appears to have two aspects or dimensions: satisfaction with service needs and satisfaction with the quality of received services. In other words, this concept of client satisfaction has two latent variables. Latent variables are abstract, and to quantify them, the researcher must develop indicators or observed variables that reflect or represent the meaning and levels of client satisfaction. The diagram in Figure 5.1 illustrates the measurement process for client satisfaction. The two circles represent two abstract dimensions or components of client satisfaction. The line connecting the circles indicates their correlation. Each circle has four squared boxes named from X1 to X8. The squared boxes represent the observed indicators of the latent variables. The arrow connecting the two latent variables indicates the correlation or covariance between them. The arrows from the latent variables to the observed indicators indicate the causal relationships between the latent variables and their respective observed indicators. Each of the arrows can be understood as a regression coefficient of an observed indicator on its respective latent

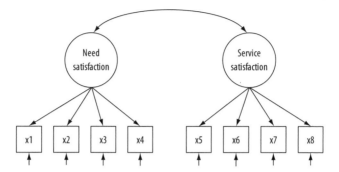

Figure 5.1 A Proposed Measurement Model of Client Satisfaction

variable. The arrows under the observed indicator boxes indicate the unique variances or measurement errors.

Reflective or Effect Indicators

The proposed measurement model in Figure 5.1 illustrates the causal relationships between latent variables and observed indicators. In measurement theory, the squares are the reflective measures of the circles. Therefore, the abstract constructs are the causes of the observed indicators (Fornell & Bookstein, 1982; Edwards & Bagozzi, 2000). The observed indicators are called reflective measures or effect indicators. The causal relationship between a construct and its indicators or measures should meet all conditions of causality. First, the construct and its indicators are two distinct phenomena. Second, the construct and its indicators must covary. Third, the construct must exist before its indicators. Finally, there should be no rival explanation for the causal relationship between the construct and its indicators (Edwards & Bagozzi, 2000).

Causal or Formative Indicators

There are situations where the observed indicators or measures are causes of latent constructs. This type of indicator is called a *formative measure* or *causal indicator* (Blalock, 1971, Bollen & Lennox, 1991; MacCullum & Browne, 1993). For example, socio-economic status can be defined as a latent construct caused by observed indicators such as education, income, job, and neighborhood (Hauser, 1973). In social work, we can

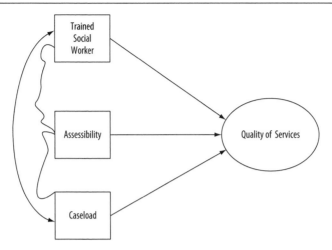

Figure 5.2 A Proposed Causal Indicator Measurement Model of Quality of Services

define, among other things, quality of social work services as the effect of availability of trained social workers, accessibility of services, and caseload.

The conventional rules of reliability and validity are not always applicable for the causal indicator measurement model (Bollen & Lennox, 1991). The measurement model in Figure 5.2 does not require that the causal indicators must be correlated as those in a *reflective indicator* model (*see* Figure 5.1). Thus, the freeform lines between "Trained social worker," "Accessibility," and "Caseload" are not specified as they are correlated. This type of causal indicator measurement model has not been used among social work researchers. Although causal indicators are theoretically meaningful, the methodology and technology to assess their measurement properties are not readily available for most researchers. Only effect indicator or reflective indicator measurement models are discussed in this book.

Measurement Process

As illustrated in Figure 5.1, to measure client satisfaction, the researcher needs to first define client satisfaction in terms of need satisfaction and service satisfaction. Then he/she must construct eight questions or items that help him/her measure the degree of client satisfaction in such as way that he/she can quantify the levels of client satisfaction from low to high. Keep in mind that the definition of an effect indicator or reflective indicator is different from the causal or formative indicator. Researchers should avoid including both effect indicators and causal indicators in one measurement model because the mixture of both effect and causal indicators can result in poor internal consistency or conceptual confusion. In theory, these eight observed variables (indicators or items) should be drawn from a finite number of observed variables. However, it is always difficult or impossible to come up with such a finite pool of observed variables for any conceivable variables. The researcher needs to link the observed variables to their respective latent dimensions (latent variables), conceptually and statistically. Conceptually, the observed items must capture the theoretical definition of the specific dimension and its overall latent variable. In this example, the four items that measure need satisfaction must reflect the meanings of need satisfaction, and the four items that measure service satisfaction must reflect service satisfaction. Statistically, the researcher must demonstrate that the four items of each dimension must correlate among themselves. Finally, a construct must be conceptualized within a theoretical framework that explains how a particular construct relates to other constructs under certain situations or circumstances. In the example of client satisfaction, the researcher might theorize that client satisfaction would relate to client's quality of life. In other words, clients seek social services to improve their quality of life. Therefore, they would only say that they were satisfied with the services if these services really improved their life situations. Having a clear theoretical framework helps researchers to conceptualize the measurement process in a more effective and meaningful way. It is always important to have a clear purpose in the attempt to construct a scale or a measurement. A theoretical framework also helps the researcher to distinguish the constructs from each other to avoid the development of an indicator that shares similar meanings with more than one construct. For example, an indicator of client satisfaction must not be an indicator of quality of life in the same situation. Constructs can also be hierarchical in their orders. For example, need satisfaction and service satisfaction are two distinct constructs but represent a higher order construct that is client satisfaction. From the confirmatory factor analysis perspective, need satisfaction and service satisfaction are the first order factors of client satisfaction

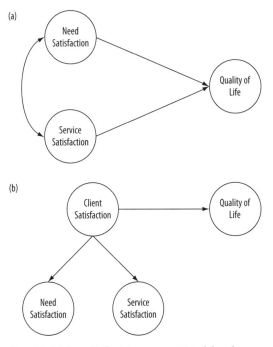

Figure 5.3 (a) First Order Measurement Model and
Theoretical Framework (b) Second Order
Measurement Model and Theoretical Framework

(*see* Figure 5.3A and Figure 5.3B). When a multidimensional scale is used
as a composite scale, it is assumed that there is a second order factor
that captures all correlated first order factors. For example, the Center
for Epidemiological Studies Depression Scale (Radloff, 1977) is conceptualized as multidimensional because it has been proven to have at least
four factors. Researchers have used it as composite scale by summing up
the scores of its 20 items to arrive to a composite score that ranges from
0 to 60. In theory, the overall score should represent a higher order factor that captures the scores of the first order factors of the scale. Finally,
having a theoretical framework helps researchers to choose appropriate
statistical approaches for data analysis.

The diagrams depicted in Figures 5.3A and 5.3B suggest that client
satisfaction has a determinant effect on quality of life. The path model
in Figure 5.3A illustrates the relationship between client satisfaction as

measured by two first order factors of need satisfaction and service satisfaction. However, in Figure 5.3B, client satisfaction is measured by a second order factor encompassing need satisfaction and service satisfaction. In both cases, improving quality of life is the expected outcome of client satisfaction.

Clearly defined concepts will help researchers and evaluators develop meaningful and appropriate indicators for what they want to measure (Bollen, 1989). It is important for social work researchers to have a clear purpose in selecting or developing a research instrument. Social work researchers and evaluators can define a research concept from existing literature or their own clinical experiences. Clinical experiences would probably provide more practical insights where there is a lack of previous research in cross-cultural settings.

Developing Measurement Indicators

Once a research problem is identified, the researcher needs to define the problem in terms of variables and constructs. After the research variables or constructs are identified and agreed upon by the research team, measurable indicators for the variables or constructs must be developed. Ideally, the indicators must be randomly drawn from a pool of all possible items, but in reality there is no such exhausted pool of items. Researchers and evaluators will have to work with what they have, given that there has been a reasonable attempt to identify the items.

In cross-cultural research and evaluation, researchers have to select the indicators or observed variables that have similar meanings across cultures. The combination of cultural expert meetings, vignette probing, and focus groups can be used to identify and construct cross-cultural instrument indicators or questions.

Cross-Cultural Expert Group Meeting

Cross-cultural expert meetings should be called to develop indicators or questions for a cross-cultural research instrument. The purposes of the expert meetings are to generate as many indicators as possible, identify the emic and etic indicators, and to develop vignettes reflecting the research aims for in-depth-interviews and key questions for focus groups. Each cultural group participating in the cross-cultural study should have at least two cultural experts, a female and a male. Recent research has suggested that men and women have different patterns of communication (Costa, 1994; Cameron, 1988). Expert members should have a good understanding of the meanings and purposes of the research aims. The experts can meet through a designated Internet "chat room," internet video conference, and face-to-face meeting. Internet chat room discussion and video conferencing should be available before and after the face-to-face meeting. Members can generate as many items for the instrument as possible before participating in a face-to-face meeting. Results from the face-to-face meeting can be discussed again over the chat room or video conference.

The results from Internet chat room, video conferences, and face-to-face meetings are combined and evaluated by the research team. All information should be archived for future evaluation and reference.

Vignette Interviews

The research team works with the cultural expert group to develop vignettes that can stimulate participants to share or reveal their experiences and insights that can help the research team identify relevant measurement indicators of the key research constructs from the prospective respondents. Vignette interviews help the researchers to *(1)* understand how people from different cultural populations understand the meanings of the research questions; *(2)* generate culturally relevant measurement indicators for the research concepts or variables; and *(3)* assist the researchers to choose the right and meaningful research questionnaire (*see* Martin, 2004). For example, if the aim of the cross-cultural research project is to compare the role of social support as a moderating factor of the negative impacts of natural disasters on psychological well-being across cultures, then the vignettes should present a hypothetical or real disaster situation that can trigger respondents' thinking about how they would cope with such a situation. The interviewer can use the vignettes to probe for the ways that respondents would react to the disasters. Through vignette probing, researchers can identify indicators of social support and psychological well-being from respondents across cultural groups. Vignette probing should be audio-recorded, transcribed, and edited for comparison and triangulation with data collected from focus and expert groups. Vignette interviews should follow the following principles:

1. Vignettes should be related the research aims and hypotheses.
2. The same vignette should be presented to members of different cultural groups.
3. At least 12 vignette interviews (6 females and 6 males) should be conducted for each cultural group. This sample size is recommended for qualitative research (Fayers & Machin, 2007).
4. Respondents should be encouraged through probing to give as many interpretations of the vignette as possible.
5. Respondents should be asked to offer their own examples in explaining their understanding of the vignettes. For example, when asking about how they would react to a disaster, interviewers should also probe the respondents to provide concrete examples either from their own experiences, imagination, or observations from people they know.

The success of vignette interviews or other types of interviews are determined by the quality of interviewers and the participants or respondents.

Information collected from vignette interviews are combined, transcribed, translated, and edited. The research team needs to compare the results from the expert group and vignette interviews to develop a preliminary list of items that will be compared with the items generated from focus group meetings.

Cross-Cultural Focus Group Meeting

Focus group methodology has been well-developed and employed in different research settings (Cote-Arsenault & Morrison-Beedy, 1999; Stewart & Shamdasami, 1990; Krueger, 1994). Well-planned focus groups can help researchers gain insight into a cultural group; develop meaningful research agendas, questions, and hypotheses; generate measurable cross-cultural indicators for research constructs or variables; and evaluate the appropriateness of research instruments.

Each cultural group participating in the cross-cultural study should have at least four to six members with equal representatives of both genders to participate in a global (all groups) cross-cultural focus meeting to identify indicators for the research instrument or questionnaire.

If it is possible, focus groups within each cultural group can be called before the global cross-cultural focus group. In each cultural or ethnic, linguistic or racial group, the team should conduct three focus groups, including two gender-specific focus groups: females (3–5 participants) vs. males (3–5 participants) and one combined gender focus group (6–12 participants with equal gender representatives). The author's experiences with focus group meeting in the Vietnamese population suggest that gender-specific focus groups provide an easy-going atmosphere for the participants to reveal their thoughts or sharing their personal experiences.

Each cultural focus group can work independently to develop as many indicators as possible. However, all groups should agree on the meanings of the research aims and definitions of key research constructs before group members work on the construction of indicators. Transcripts from these meetings should be translated into a common language when the groups are from different linguistic populations.

Data Synthesis

Once the research team compiles data from experts, vignette interviews, and focus groups, the research team needs to synthesize the data to produce a comprehensive list of meaningful items that are both relevant to the research aims and culturally appropriate to all participating cultural groups. The next step is to put together a preliminary research questionnaire or instrument for further evaluation.

Instrument Form

Once there is a list of acceptable and meaningful indicators for the research constructs, the team will have to decide on the appropriate structure and form for these indicators (Schaeffer & Presser, 2003). The most convenient and practical way of measuring human behaviors, attitudes, mental status, opinions, and other aspects life is by asking questions. As researchers attempt to measure human behaviors for theory building, theory testing, policy-making, or evaluation of treatment efficacy, they must ask the right questions to get the right data for their answers. Fortunately, questionnaire development has become more scientific, with proven effective methods for asking questions. Schaeffer and

Presser (2003) have noted that survey researchers often focus on two types of questions: "questions about events or behaviors and questions that ask for evaluations or attitudes" (p. 65). The research indicators or variables can be framed as "open" or "closed" questions. Each type has advantages and disadvantages. For example, open questioning allows the researchers to collect more in-depth and current information from the respondents, but they are less efficient in terms of data management and analysis. Open questions have the "ability to capture answers unanticipated by questionnaire designers" (Martin, 2006, p .6). Closed questions are more efficient but can miss important information because of the lack of well-defined categories. Schwartz and Oysrman (2001) offered a good review on the types of questionnaire response formats and their advantages and disadvantages. There is no perfect response format for any research instrument; the researchers will have to choose those that are feasible and meaningful for different cross-cultural settings.

Survey methodologists have suggested several standardized techniques for questionnaire development (Converse & Pressner, 1986; Schaeffer & Pressner, 2003). An effective survey instrument must satisfy some basic conditions, as suggested by Fowler and Cannell (1996). Followings are six criteria for good survey questionnaire design:

1. The questions must be culturally relevant to respondents of diverse cultural backgrounds.
2. Respondents must understand the intention of the questions.
3. Researchers must avoid asking questions for information that is not available to the respondents.
4. Respondents must be able to recall or retrieve information relevant to the questions.
5. Respondents can translate the information they have into the standardized forms of the questions.
6. Respondents' answers to the questions must be truthful and accurate.

Although these six basic principles of instrument development appear to be simple and common sense, researchers should remember that these principles do not offer a perfect solution for instrument development. They are useful criteria and should be adapted as the guide for research instrument construction. For respondents to understand the true meanings of questions, items, or statements, they must be written in a clear and precise language. The language of a research instrument must be free from gender, age, educational, racial, and religious biases. Researchers should avoid questions that require respondents to search for the information that is not readily available or information that they are not accustomed to remembering. For example, in a society where people do not celebrate their birthday (e.g., rural villages in Vietnam), it will be very difficult for the researchers to ask the respondents to provide information about their parents' or siblings' birthday. If this is an important question for the research project, then respondents should be informed in advance or allowed adequate time to get or retrieve the information.

Standardized formats for research instrument questions can be found in most basic textbooks of research methodology (DeVellis, 1991; Fayers & Machin, 2007). Members of the research team, experts, and prospective participants should agree on which standardized question formats or scale formats are suitable for the research project. The formats or forms and the contents of the questions and answers must be easily understood and familiar to the respondents for them to provide appropriate responses to the questions.

Cross-Cultural Evaluation

Once a pool of items is developed and compiled into a preliminary questionnaire or a research instrument, it is subjected to a series of cross-cultural evaluation. Four approaches of cross-cultural evaluation are described: cultural expert evaluation, cognitive interviews, focus groups, and pilot testing.

Cultural Expert Evaluation

The purpose of cultural expert evaluation is to seek consensus among the cultural experts representing the selected cultural or racial/ethnic groups on the cultural validity and equivalence of the newly developed instrument. Expert appraisal has been found as an effective means of survey questionnaire evaluation (Lessler & Forsyth, 1996; Forsyth, Levin & Fisher, 1999). Researchers can use the same expert group that worked on the development of the instrument items or recruit a new group to engage in the evaluation of the newly developed instrument. This task of evaluation can be performed through Internet chat rooms, video conferences, E-mails, and a face-to-face meeting. If it is possible, a face-to-face meeting should be arranged for all participating cultural experts to evaluate the contents and format of the newly developed instrument. Members of this cultural expert group should be comprised of professionals from the target populations and should have appropriate training and clinical experiences concerning the problem under investigation. The experts are asked to evaluate at least four aspects of each research item in the instrument: conceptual, clarity, appropriateness, and difficulty.

The evaluation matrix presented in Table 5.1 can be used as a part of expert evaluation. It can enhance the data collected from expert focus group meetings or discussion via other forms of electronic communication. This evaluation matrix can also be used with cognitive interviews and focus groups as a means of collecting additional standardized data for the overall evaluation of the instrument.

Conceptual

Committee members evaluate the conceptual linkage between the suggested items and their respective research ideas or variables. The key issue is whether the suggested items reflect the meanings of the concepts that they are supposed to represent.

Clarity

Committee members evaluate the use of words and syntax of the item. Can respondents from different cultural backgrounds clearly understand the item or question in a similar manner? Is the item written in a manner that is free from jargons or parochial idioms?

Appropriateness

Committee members determine whether the suggested items are culturally appropriate in each cultural group. Does the item or question require information that is taboo for some cultures or can it induce embarrassment for the participants?

Difficulty

Committee members determine whether the suggested items are difficult for prospective respondents or participants to understand and respond

Table 5.1 Item Evaluation Matrix

	Member 1		Member 2		Member 3	
	Yes	No[a]	Yes	No	Yes	No
Item 1						
Conceptual						
Clarity						
Appropriateness						
Difficulty						
Item 2						
Conceptual						
Clarity						
Appropriateness						
Difficulty						
Item 3						
Conceptual						
Clarity						
Appropriateness						
Difficulty						
Item k						
Conceptual						
Clarity						
Appropriateness						
Difficulty						

[a]If the evaluation is No, committee members must provide a written explanation and rationale.

to. Does the item require respondents to spend a lot of time to think or gather information?

Cognitive Interviews

Researchers have suggested that cognitive interviews should be used to evaluate the research questionnaire (Rothgeb, Willis & Forsyth, 2005). Cognitive interviewing is designed to identify potential sources of measurement errors in research instruments or questionnaires (O'Brien, Fisher, Goldenberg, & Rosen, 2001). This method can be used to

(1) appraise respondents' comprehension of each question or item in a research instruments; *(2)* judge the consistency of respondents' comprehension; and *(3)* evaluate the congruency between respondents' comprehension and the researchers' intention (Collins, 2003).

Self-reporting questionnaires or data collection instruments are "highly context dependent" (Schwartz & Oyserman, 2001). In cross-cultural research settings, the self-reporting data collection instruments are also highly cultural- and linguistic-dependent. This suggests that the ways that researchers construct their data collection instruments will definitely influence the data they obtain. The ultimate goal of the research instruments is to collect the correct data for the research purposes. Unfortunately, previous research has revealed that respondents or participants often do not provide the quality data the researchers intended to gather through their research instruments (Schwartz & Oyserman, 2001).

It is not a simple task to construct a question or a measurement item that exhibits the same meanings for all people. This problem becomes even greater in cross-cultural research. Therefore, the evaluation of the research instruments prior to data collection is crucially important for the success of the research project. One of the best ways to assess the quality of a research instrument is to directly ask the respondents how they understand the meanings of the research instruments and whether their comprehension truly reflects the researchers' intentions. Cognitive interviewing has been used as a "pretesting" approach to detect potential errors in cross-cultural questionnaire development (Agans, Deeb-Sossa, & Kalsbeek, 2006).

The principles of a cognitive interview are based on the four-stage cognitive process of respondents or participants. This process encompasses the respondents' ability to *(1)* understand the information presented to them; *(2)* retrieve relevant information; *(3)* evaluate the information; and *(4)* communicate the information (O'Brien, Fisher, Goldenberg, & Rosen, 2001). When respondents are presented the items of the questionnaire, they are expected to be able to understand the meanings of the items, to retrieve any relevant information or knowledge related to the items, to judge or evaluate the content of the items, and to communicate their attitudes, thoughts, or feelings concerning the meaning, relevancy, and appropriateness of the items by choosing the right answers presented to them in the closed questions (e.g., very happy, somewhat happy, or not happy).

There are two approaches to cognitive interviewing: the think-aloud approach and verbal probing. Each has advantages and disadvantages (Willis, 1999). Researchers can use both approaches simultaneously. Cognitive interviews can be conducted in a laboratory or in the field. For a cross-cultural research project, it is suggested that cognitive interviews be conducted in the field to reflect the "real-life" situations of the participants. The think-aloud approach is straightforward; the interviewers read the item or question from the questionnaire and ask the participant to tell what he/she is thinking about. The verbal probing approach requires the interviewers to ask more related questions to extract detailed information from the participants on a specific item or question.

The preparation for a cognitive interview includes the following steps:

1. **Recruiting and training interviewers**. Although cognitive interviewing requires minimum interview training, the research team should recruit interviewers who are culturally and linguistically competent to carry out successful interviews. Interviewers should practice reading the items or questions of the questionnaire several times before engaging in the interviews. Interviewers and participants should be the same sex. This would create a more "comfortable" zone of interaction between interviewers and interviewees. Interviewers must be trained to have a good understanding of the purpose of the research, the meanings of the research questionnaire and its items, and the skills to probe for in-depth answers and encourage the participants to reveal their thoughts and feelings about each item of the questionnaire. Interviewers should frame the interview questions around four aspects: conceptual, clarity, appropriateness, and difficulty.

2. **Recruiting and training participants**. Six to twelve cognitive interviews should be conducted for each cultural group. An equal number of female and male respondents must be the rule in all evaluation processes. Before an interview, participants should be trained to be familiar with the interviewing process; for example, they should listen to each question carefully and communicate their thoughts about the questions freely. Participants should also be prepared to respond to the additional probing willingly.

3. **Having the right equipment for data collection.** Digital recording technology is an ideal means of verbal data recording, as it allows the researchers to conduct longer interviews (several hours of interviewing without interruptions), transfer interviewing data to PC, and save interviewing data into different folders.

To improve the quality of the data, all participants should have the full instrument in their own language to review at least 1 week prior to the interview. The more they are familiar with the instrument, the better they can provide their thoughtful assessment of the instrument. Traditional qualitative interview techniques can be used for cognitive interviews (Berg, 2004). Interviewers must be fluent in the language of the participants and also should have an adequate knowledge about the culture of the participants.

In addition to in-depth information from cognitive interviewing, the evaluation matrix presented in Table 5.1 can be used to collect additional quantitative data for the evaluation purposes. This evaluation matrix allows researchers to collect additional quantitative data to compliment the qualitative data of cognitive interviews.

Focus Group

Focus groups are used to assess the cultural validity of the pool of possible indicators generated by experts and participants from the vignette interviews. The procedure and techniques of focus group methods have been well discussed in the literature (Morgan, 1988). The research team should list all key research concepts and their respective indicators and make them available to all invited focus group participants at least 1 week prior to the meeting. There should be two types of focus group: within- and between (global)- focus groups. Let's say that a social work researcher wishes to study the prevalence of depression in Latino and Asian-American communities. These two broad ethnic populations encompass several subgroups that have their own culture, values, and languages. It would be imprudent to assume that these subgroups have a similar cultural background, and depression bears the same meaning and manifestation among these groups. The researcher can approach this problem by creating a multicultural advisory group that serves as a means to screen and synthesize cultural similarities among the selected groups. The research team should conduct at least three focus groups for each ethnic group. Two focus groups should be gender-specific and the third is the combination of both gender groups. Considering gender differences in the process of measurement development is an effective way to avoid gender biases in both measurement and outcomes.

Data Synthesis

Evaluation data from expert groups, cognitive interviews, and focus groups will be synthesized to provide a comprehensive and in-depth assessment of the preliminary research questionnaire or instrument. This task can take several days because of the labor-intensive demand of the interview transcriptions, translation, and data analysis. Once the research team agrees on the final draft of the questionnaire, it is ready to be tested in the field.

Pilot Testing

A pilot-structured interview via a purposive survey is conducted to test the cross-cultural research questionnaire developed from experts, cognitive interviews, and focus groups. If possible, telephone interviews, face-to-face interviews, and mail-surveys can be used simultaneously to improve the validity of the questionnaire. A reliable and valid questionnaire should produce similar data regardless of the data collection methods. The sample size of the pilot survey test is determined by the number of items of the selected scale or instrument. From the factor analysis perspective, each item of a scale requires the minimum number of five subjects. A 20-item scale would require a sample of at least 100 subjects from each participant group for a reliability validity evaluation via Cronbach's α-analysis and factor analysis. Random sampling is always a desirable method to draw a sample, but it is often not feasible. Therefore, the research team should make every effort to recruit individuals from diverse backgrounds of the target population to participate in the pilot test.

With the data from the pilot survey, researchers can use different statistical approaches to assess the cross-cultural validity and reliability of the research instruments. Chapter 6 will demonstrate the applications of some basic statistical techniques to evaluate the cross-cultural equivalence of the research instruments.

6

Assessing Measurement Equivalence

T his chapter illustrates four descriptive statistical approaches to evaluating the cross-cultural equivalence of the research instruments:
data distribution of the items of the research instrument, the patterns
of responses of each item, the corrected item–total correlation, and
exploratory factor analysis (EFA).

In comparative research (whether it is cross-cultural, cross-national
or multi-group comparisons), the assumption of measurement equivalence is crucially important. If non-equivalent measures were used, the
outcomes would be seriously biased (Hui & Triandis, 1985; Poortinga,
1989). Equivalence is the fundamental issue in cross-cultural research
and evaluation. Poortinga (1989) argued that a cross-cultural comparison can be misleading for two reasons: *(1)* comparison was made
by using different attributes and *(2)* comparison was made by using
different scale units. But even when the problems of equivalence in
attributes and scale units are resolved, it does not warrant a valid cross-
cultural comparison. One should approach the equivalence issues in
cross-cultural research through the entire research process (van Herk,
Poortinga & Verhallen, 2003). In every step of the research process, the
researcher must ensure that equivalence in concept, operationalization,
methods, analysis, and interpretation receive the same attention.

General Issues in Cross-Cultural Equivalence Comparison

From methodological perspectives, there are at least four general issues of cross-cultural equivalence: conceptual, measurement, data, and analysis. Conceptual equivalence requires that a concept or variable be defined similarly across cultural groups. Measurement equivalence requires that the research instruments used to collect data for the defined variables bear the same meanings and psychometric properties. Data equivalence requires that data be collected in the same manner across cultural groups, such as the use of the same sampling designs and data collection techniques (i.e., telephone interviews, face-to-face interviews, or mail survey). Equivalence of analysis requires that the same statistical methods be used for the data across groups. For example, if one wants to compare gender differences in depression among three ethnic groups, then it is assumed that depression is defined similarly and understood by subjects among the three comparative ethnic groups, a depression scale that has similar psychometric properties among the three groups is used, and data on depression are collected using the same sampling designs and data collection techniques, and one statistical test such as a t-test is used to compare mean differences in depression between females and males among the three groups.

This chapter will focus on the use of descriptive statistics, reliability analysis, and factor analysis as the preliminary and descriptive techniques to ascertain cross-cultural equivalence of selected measurements for researchers who are not familiar with more advanced methods of cross-cultural measurement equivalence evaluations. Concrete examples from existing research will be used to elucidate the process and procedure of cross-cultural equivalence evaluation. Table 6.1 highlights the major tasks of cross-cultural evaluation of research instruments.

Research Designs

All comparative studies should employ similar sampling designs, data collection techniques, and data analysis procedures. Details of the research designs should be listed side by side for all research populations or groups, including the procedures used to develop sampling frames, sample size estimates, and power analysis.

Table 6.1 Cross-Cultural Equivalence Tasks

Equivalence analysis	Evaluation criteria
Research designs	Similar design issues
Descriptive analysis	Data distribution, response pattern
Reliability analysis	Corrected item–total correlation
Exploratory factor analysis (CFA)	Factor pattern
Confirmatory factor analysis (CFA)	Factor pattern, factor loadings
	Measurement errors
	Goodness of fit
Multigroup CFA	Compare measurement properties

Descriptive Analysis

Descriptive analysis requires the researcher to evaluate the shape of data distribution and the pattern of responses for each item of a scale or an instrument between the comparative groups. Differences in data distribution and pattern of responses of the instrument items are early signs of differences in reliability and validity of the research instrument between the comparative groups. In the following example, nine items of the Center for Epidemiologic Studies Depression Scale (CESD) scale were evaluated across four samples: White-American, African-American, Japanese and Russian. These samples represent two levels of cross-cultural research: racial comparison within one nation and racial and national comparison between two nations and languages. The sources of data were discussed in Chapter 1. Following is the description of the items.

1. I felt **depressed**.
2. I felt that everything I did was an **effort**.
3. My **sleep** was restless.
4. I felt **lonely**.
5. People were **unfriendly**.
6. I did not feel like **eating**; my appetite was poor.
7. I felt **sad**.
8. I felt that people **dislike** me.
9. I could not get "**going**."

Data Distribution

Equivalence in data distribution of the items

This matter is verified by an analysis of the shape of the item distribution. The SPSS procedures of DESCRIPTIVE and FREQUENCIES provide the statistics in Tables 6.2 and 6.3. The scores of the item ranged from 1 to 3 in all samples. This is important because different scoring patterns produce different means and shapes for the data. Two important statistics in Table 6.2 that need to be examined and compared across groups are the kurtosis and skewness. Skewness is a measure of symmetry. If the distribution of the data on a particular item is normally distributed, its scores spread out equally in both sides of its mean. Kurtosis indicates whether the distribution of an item is peaked or flat relative to a normal distribution (*NIST/SEMATECH e-Handbook of Statistical Methods*, http://www.itl.nist.gov/div898/handbook/, 2008). In the context of measurement equivalence assessment, we expect that the skewness and kurtosis of each item of a scale or an index have similar values or distribution shapes across the comparative groups. Differences in the values of skewness and kurtosis suggest nonequivalence in psychometric properties, such as reliability and factor loadings.

Among the four samples, the African-American sample seems to have more items (seven of nine) that have values of skewness that approach 0. There are only three items in the White sample that have values of skewness that approach 0. None of the items in the Japanese

Table 6.2 Skewness and Kurtosis of Nine CESD Items Across Four Cultural Groups

Item	Whites ($n = 1135$)		African-Americans ($n = 496$)		Japanese ($n = 2180$)		Russians ($n = 299$)	
	Skew	Kurtosis	Skew	Kurtosis	Skew	Kurtosis	Skew	Kurtosis
Depressed	1.19	0.415	0.80	−0.40	3.10	9.33	1.12	−0.43
Effort	0.85	−0.34	0.46	−1.04	2.36	4.29	0.97	−0.72
Sleep	0.54	−0.85	0.62	−0.81	2.01	3.26	0.76	−1.12
Lonely	1.38	0.86	0.94	−0.24	2.41	5.27	1.24	−0.17
Unfriendly	2.83	7.44	1.84	2.46	5.34	30.60	2.67	6.18
Eating	1.38	1.94	0.93	−0.34	3.10	9.65	2.22	3.53
Sad	1.30	0.67	0.87	−0.249	2.97	8.60	1.31	0.21
Dislike	3.27	10.65	2.21	4.18	6.71	48.20	2.18	3.32
Going	0.70	−0.474	0.56	−0.77	2.69	6.74	1.66	1.27

Table 6.3 Pattern of Item Responses: African-American, White, Japanese, and Russian

Items	Responses (%)		
	Hardly ever	Sometime	Most of the time
I felt depressed.			
African-American	54.8	37.3	**7.9**
White	66.1	29.4	**4.5**
Japanese	87.7	9.2	**2.1**
Russian	67.6	14.4	18.1
Everything was an effort.			
African-American	43.7	39.0	**17.3**
White	56.9	34.0	**9.1**
Japanese	83.4	13.9	**2.6**
Russian	63.5	17.4	19.1
Sleep was restless.			
African-American	48.8	37.7	13.6
White	46.1	40.2	13.7
Japanese	80.0	17.4	*2.7*
Russian	58.9	18.4	22.7
I felt lonely.			
African-American	58.6	32.6	8.9
White	69.2	25.1	5.7
Japanese	84.3	13.7	*2.0*
Russian	70.6	12.0	17.4
People were unfriendly.			
African-American	77.0	18.3	4.7
White	87.0	10.0	3.0
Japanese	95.6	3.7	*0.7*
Russian	86.0	9.4	4.7
Didn't feel like eating.			
African-American	58.3	31.3	10.5
White	75.4	18.5	6.0
Japanese	88.9	9.2	*1.9*
Russian	82.9	9.0	8.0
I felt sad.			
African-American	57.6	36.2	6.3
White	67.9	27.3	4.8
Japanese	88.3	10.1	*1.6*
Russian	69.2	17.7	13.0

(*continued*)

Table 6.3 Pattern of Item Responses: African-American, White, Japanese, and Russian (*continued*)

Items	Responses (%)		
	Hardly ever	*Sometime*	*Most of the time*
I felt people disliked me.			
African-American	81.8	15.0	3.2
White	89.7	8.6	1.7
Japanese	97.1	2.2	0.7
Russian	82.6	9.0	8.4
I couldn't get going.			
African-American	46.4	41.5	12.1
White	53.2	40.6	**6.2**
Japanese	86.1	11.4	**2.5**
Russian	75.6	13.7	10.7

sample has a value of skewness approaching 0. Overall, all of the skewness values in the four samples are significantly large. This situation is more obvious in the Japanese sample.

With respect to the Kurtosis values, the items "people were unfriendly" and "I felt people dislike me" have greater values compare to other items in all samples. However they are more extreme in the Japanese (30.60 and 48.20) and White (7.44 and 10.65) samples than in the African-American sample (2.460 and 4.180). The Russian sample appears to have the least skewed data for the CESD items compared to the data of the other three samples. We will see that difference in data distribution of the items can affect the reliability of the scale among these comparative samples.

Pattern of Responses

The next step is the examination of the pattern of responses for each item across the samples. This descriptive analysis can provide some preliminary information on how individuals from different cultural groups respond to a specific question or item of a scale or an instrument. Table 6.3 presents the patterns of responses of nine CESD items across four samples. The results reveal significant cross-cultural differences in patterns of item responses, especially in the category of 'Most Time."

There was the smallest percentage of Japanese respondents in this category.

Internal Consistency Analysis

This analysis is based on the average correlation of all items on the scale. The higher the average correlation among the items is, the higher the internal consistency. Cronbach's α-coefficient is the summary statistic of how well the items of a scale "tie" together in measuring an overall construct or variable. If a researcher develops a measure of depression that is comprised of nine items, these scale items must correlate highly among themselves because they are supposed to measure the same construct of depression. Examining the pattern of "corrected item–total correlation" can shed light on potential cross-cultural biases in the reliability of the selected measure. In this example, a SPSS-based reliability analysis was used to illustrate this procedure. The analysis includes the specification of a reliability model that is α, item statistics, and item–total statistics. The most important outcomes that need to be interpreted are the item–total correlation statistics. This statistic allows the researcher to identify which item of a scale has good or poor correlation with the sum of all items on the scale. It tells the researchers how well a particular item correlates with all other items of a scale. The results in Table 6.4 reveal that all but two items in the Russian sample have the greater correlation with the overall scale compared to other samples. Seven of nine items in the Russian sample have a correlation greater than 0.50 compared to four in the Japanese sample, four in the White sample, and five in the African-American sample. As a result, the Russian sample has the largest Cronbach's α-coefficient compared to other samples. These results are related to the findings in Tables 6.2 and 6.3. The nine selected CESD items in the Russian sample appear to be less skewed with smoother response pattern than those of the other samples. So far, all of the results tend to indicate that these items have weak cross-cultural equivalence in their psychometric properties.

It should be noted that the results in Table 6.4 reveal that all nine items in the sample of Russian have relatively greater corrected item–total correlation coefficients than the other groups. Consequently, the α-coefficient of internal consistency reliability is also greater in the sample of Russian than in the other three samples. Different values of

Table 6.4 Corrected Item–Total Correlation and Cronbach's α

Items	African-American	White	Japanese	Russian
I felt depressed.	0.606	0.624	0.584	0.724
Everything was an effort.	0.498	0.503	0.548	0.573
Sleep was restless.	0.517	0.370	0.406	0.461
I felt lonely.	0.623	0.530	0.580	0.615
People were unfriendly.	0.358	0.325	0.448	0.525
I didn't feel like eating.	0.443	0.398	0.454	0.385
I felt sad.	0.642	0.562	0.499	0.714
I felt people disliked me.	0.422	0.353	0.353	0.581
I couldn't get going.	0.579	0.484	0.552	0.639
Cronbach's α	0.820	0.775	0.796	0.853

corrected item–total correlation coefficients across the four groups indicate that the measure of depression lacks cross-cultural equivalence in reliability.

Exploratory Factor Analysis

Factor analysis has been used to evaluate the validity of research instruments. This statistical method allows researchers to identify the dimensions of a latent construct via the covariance structure of the items used to measure the construct. Factor analysis can be used as a tool to identify the underlying dimensions of a set of variables or items designed to measure a construct such as self-esteem or depression. The method provides information on the relationship between an item and its respective latent dimension (factor) of a unidimensional or multidimensional construct (Child, 1990). There are some basic requirements for the use of factor analysis:

Data should be collected randomly.
Items should be measured on interval or ratio level of measurement.
Items should have univariate and bivariate distribution shape.
Items should have multivariate normality.

In reality, these assumptions are often ignored. However, there are some conditions that must be observed carefully, including adequate sample size and sufficient number of items for each respective factor. The rule of thumb is each item should have at least 10 cases or 10 observations. If a scale has 10 items, researchers need a minimum of 100 cases or observations to arrive at meaningful results (Nunnally, 1978; Pedhazur & Schmelkin, 1991). In addition, each factor should have from three to five items, and it cannot have less than two items (Bentler, 1976; Kim & Mueller, 1978).

There is also confusion between the use of principal component analysis (PCA) and EFA. As Costello and Osborne (2005) noted that "PCA is not a true method of factor analysis and there is disagreement among statistical theorists about when it should be used" (pp. 1–2). They suggest that "factor analysis is preferable to principal component analysis" because PCA "is only a data reduction method," whereas "the aim of factor analysis is to reveal any latent variables that cause the manifest variables to covary" (p. 2). Many social work researchers are familiar with SPSS for their data analysis. Principal component analysis is the default method extraction in SPSS. Therefore, to avoid using PCA in the evaluation of cross-cultural equivalence of the factor structure of a selected scale or instrument, one should consider using other methods of factor extraction, including unweighted least squares, generalized least squares, maximum likelihood, principal axis factoring, α-factoring, or image factoring.

Fabrigar, Wegener, MacCallum, and Strahan (1999) suggest that maximum likelihood be used when the data approach normal distribution. This method offers several measures of goodness-of-fit for the factor model as well as tests of statistical significance. When data are not normally distributed, principal axis factoring should be used. Although SPSS offer six factor extraction methods as listed before, maximum likelihood and principal axis factoring are considered the best choice because they would provide the best solutions (Costello & Osborne, 2005).

The data presented in Tables 6.2 and 6.3 reveal that the nine CESD items are not normally distributed across the four samples. Therefore, principal axis factoring should be the best choice for the evaluation of the cross-cultural equivalence in the factor structure of the nine CESD items. These nine items should be considered to have cross-cultural equivalence across the four selected samples representing cultural, racial, ethnic, and national differences when they meet the following conditions:

1. Having the same number of factors or latent variables across the selected comparative groups
2. Having the same factor loadings for each factor across the selected comparative groups

Other assumptions that should be considered are:

1. Using similar sampling methods
2. Using similar data collection methods
3. Items are measured on the same numerical scale

The results of the EFAs for the nine CESD items across the samples of African-American, White, Japanese, and Russian are based on the following factor analysis procedures:

1. Factor extraction: principal axis factoring
2. Rotation method: varimax with Kaiser Normalization

The role of rotation procedure in factor analysis is to produce a clearer structure of the items. Factor rotation is necessary to provide the interpretability of the factor structure. Once the numbers of factors are extracted from the data, one needs to determine the relationships among the factors. Orthogonal rotation produces a set of factors that are independent from each other, whereas oblique rotation produces the correlated factors (Thompson, 2004). For example, if a factor analysis was performed with 10 items, 5 items were designed to measure self-esteem and the other 5 to measure life satisfaction. The orthogonal rotation would be the best procedure because it would produce a two-independent-factor model with one for self-esteem and the other for life satisfaction. SPSS can produce five rotation methods as follows (*see* SPSS, 2007). Varimax method is an orthogonal rotation method that minimizes the number of variables that have high loadings on each factor and simplifies the interpretation of the factors. Direct oblimin method produces intercorrelated factors. Quartimax method minimizes the number of factors needed to explain each variable. Equamax method is a combination of the varimax method, which simplifies the factors, and the quartimax method, which simplifies the variables. Promax rotation allows factors to be correlated and is useful for large data sets. Among the five rotation methods listed, varimax method is considered the most useful method because it produces factors that are uncorrelated (Costello & Osborne, 2005).

Table 6.5 Exploratory Factor Analysis for Cross-Cultural Equivalence of Factor Structures

Items	White		African-American			Japanese		Russian	
	F1	F2	F1	F2	D	F1	F2	F1	F2
I felt depressed.	0.725		0.659		0.066	0.638		0.477	0.654
Everything was an effort.	0.564		0.575		0.011	0.662			0.822
Sleep was restless.	0.414		0.539		0.125	0.440		0.301	0.391
I felt lonely.	0.568		0.664		0.096	0.434	0.503	0.695	
People were unfriendly.		0.685		0.591	0.094	0.707	0.522		
I didn't feel like eating.	0.417		0.469		0.052	0.519			0.441
I felt sad.	0.622		0.662		0.040	0.323	0.516	0.839	
I felt people dislike me.		0.508		0.704	0.196	0.446	0.650		
I couldn't get going.	0.531		0.621		0.090	0.495	0.375	0.556	0.415

The results of a cross-cultural equivalence analysis of the factor structure of the nine CESD items are presented in Table 6.5. Note that in this table only those factor loadings that are greater than 0.30 are retained. Tabachnick and Fidell (2001) suggested a value of 0.32 as the minimum value for a factor loading. In Table 6.5, the D column delineates the absolute difference in the value of the factor loadings between the groups. For example, the difference of the factor loading of item "I felt depressed" between the Whites and African-Americans is 0.066 (0.727–0.659 = 0.066). A difference of 0.05 or greater could be a sign of a potential lack of cross-cultural equivalence.

Factor Pattern Comparison

The first level of analysis and interpretation is factor pattern comparison. For a scale or instrument to have cross-cultural equivalence among the comparative groups, it must exhibit the same pattern of factor structure among the groups. In general the factor analysis produces two factor solutions in all four groups but the values of factor loadings are different across groups, especially in the Japanese and Russian samples. In the White and African-American samples, the factor pattern and the values of factor loadings are somewhat similar—that is, the items loaded on their respective factor similarly between the two groups. The same seven items loaded on the first factor, and the same two items loaded on the second factor. This is not true in the Japanese and Russian samples. In the Japanese sample, the items "I felt lonely" and "I felt sad" have acceptable factor loadings on both factors. In the Russian sample, the items "I felt depressed," "sleep was restless," and "I couldn't get going" have acceptable factor loadings on both factors.

The conclusions of factor pattern comparison are:

1. There is equivalence in the factor pattern of the nine CESD items between Whites and African-Americans. However, the factor loadings indicate weak equivalence between the two groups.
2. There is no equivalence in the factor pattern of the nine CESD items among Whites, Japanese, and Russians and similarly among African-Americans, Japanese, and Russians.
3. There is no cross-cultural equivalence in the factor pattern between Japanese and Russians.
4. There is no cross-national and cross-cultural equivalence among Americans, Japanese and the Russians.

Factor Loading Comparison

Once the researchers establish the equivalence in the factor pattern, the
next step is to compare the equivalence of factor loadings. The results
in Table 6.5 suggest that factor pattern of the nine CESD items is similar between the White and African-American samples. However, the
"absolute values" of difference in the factor loadings in the D column of
Table 6.5 indicate that there are five items that have different factor loadings between the samples; the items "sleep was restless" and "I felt people
dislike me" have a significantly greater factor loading in the African-
American sample. However, these differences are not profound. The
following analyses illustrate the outcomes of cross-cultural comparisons
of depression between older African-Americans and Whites.

Within-Nation Cross-Cultural Comparison: Subgroup Analysis of Depression, Life
Satisfaction, and Physical Activities between Older African-Americans and Whites

The purpose of this analysis is to illustrate that when a scale has an
acceptable level of equivalence between the comparison groups, the pattern of the relationship between the outcome variables and predictor
variables should be similar regardless of the configuration of the outcome
variable. In addition, the example illustrates that minimum differences in
the factor loadings will not affect the outcomes of comparisons. Analyses of correlation between three configurations of the depression and life
satisfaction are performed within each group. In these analyses, the first
depression scale consisted of all nine items with different factor loadings
between groups. The second depression scale consisted of five items that
exhibited differences in factor loadings, and the third depression scale
consisted of four items that had very similar factor loadings between
African-Americans and Whites. Table 6.6 presents the results of these
analyses.

Table 6.6 Impacts of Differences in Factor Loadings and Cronbach's α

	Nine CESD items			Five CESD items			Four CESD items		
	African-American	White	D	African-American	White	D	African-American	White	D
Life satisfaction[a]	0.244	0.385	0.140	0.183	0.347	0.164	0.256	0.350	0.094
Cronbach's α	0.820	0.775	0.045	0.683	0.584	0.099	0.691	0.693	0.002

Note: [a]Higher score of life satisfaction scale refers to poorer level of satisfaction.

The 9-CESD items analysis reveals that the correlation between life satisfaction and depression is lower for African-Americans ($r = 0.244$) compared to Whites ($r = 0.385$). However, the Cronbach's α is greater for African-Americans (0.820) than Whites (0.775). Can we conclude that life satisfaction has a greater influence on depression for Whites than for African-Americans-? The answer is no, because the depression scale lacks of factor loading equivalence and reliability equivalence.

When the five items that have greater differences in factor loadings and Cronbach's α were used, the difference between African-Americans ($r = 0.183$) and Whites ($r = 0.347$) becomes even greater, as reported under column D of Table 6.6.

However, when only items that have equivalent factor loadings are used, the racial difference on the impact of life satisfaction on depression between African-Americans ($r = 0.256$) and Whites ($r = 0.350$) becomes significantly smaller. Although the cross-cultural or racial comparison of depression between African-Americans and Whites are based on different configurationa of the depression scale, conceptually, the results in Table 6.6 help us to understand of the consequences of the use of nonequivalent research scales or instruments.

Within- and Between-Nation Comparisons

The following example as presented in Table 6.7 illustrates both within- and between-nation comparisons of factor patterns of nine CESD items.

Cross-cultural comparisons can be made at difference levels. We can use the familiar terms of micro and macro in social work as the guide for making cross-cultural comparisons. Microlevel of cross-cultural comparisons is comparison of within-cultural differences based on sex, economic status, religion, language, and racial and ethnic identity. Macrolevel of cross-cultural comparisons involves societies and nations. From the analysis presented in Table 6.7, one can make the following cross-cultural comparisons:

1. Gender comparison within each nation
2. Gender comparison between two nations
3. Single gender comparison between nations

If there were equivalences in the factor structure of the nine CESD items, the aforementioned results should be the same or approximately similar

Table 6.7 Exploratory Factor Analysis for Cross-Cultural Equivalence of Factor Structures

| | American | | | | | Japanese | | | | |
| | Male | | Female | | D | Male | | Female | | D |
	F1	F2	F1	F2		F1	F2	F1	F2	
I felt depressed.	0.671		0.716		0.045	0.564		0.620		0.056
Everything was an effort.	0.607		0.558		0.*049*	0.561		0.737		0.*176*
Sleep was restless.	0.500		0.417		0.083	0.477		0.402		0.075
I felt lonely.	0.603		0.599		0.004	0.523		**0.362**	**0.582**	
People were unfriendly.		0.548		0.615	0.*067*		0.840		0.619	0.*222*
I didn't feel like eating.	0.533		0.422		0.111	0.471		0.538		0.067
I felt sad.	**0.583**	**0.336**	0.648			**0.382**	**0.349**		0.655	
I felt people dislike me.		0.698		0.626	0.072		0.461		0.404	0.057
I couldn't get going.	0.574		0.551		0.023	0.471		**0.514**	**0.423**	

Extraction method: principal axis factoring.
Rotation method: varimax with Kaiser normalization.

for men and women in both within- and between-nation comparisons. However, the results from the EFA in Table 6.7 clearly indicate that there are gender differences in the factor structure of the nine CESD items. The differences can be found in both within- and between-nation comparisons.

Consequences of Nonequivalent Measurement

The following example illustrates the consequences of using an outcome measure that lacks cultural equivalence in the validity and reliability. The nine-CESD-item scale was created by summing up these nine items, and an independent t-test was used to compare gender difference in depression and Pearson's correlation of age and depression for both within- and between-nation comparisons. The results are presented in Table 6.8.

Table 6.8 Consequences of Measurement Nonequivalence in Cross-Cultural Research: National and Racial Differences in Sex, Age, and Depression

		Japanese data		American data	
		n	Mean	n	Mean
Depression	Men	938	9.89	528	12.36
	Women	1128	10.36	1067	12.97
T-values		-5.158^{a}		-3.432^{a}	
(r) Depression and age		0.064^{b}		0.090^{b}	

$^{a} p = 0.001,\ ^{b} p = 0.01$

The results presented in Table 6.8 suggest that for within-nation comparisons, both Japanese women and American women reported a slightly higher level of depression than men. For between-nation comparisons, both American men and American women reported a significantly higher level of depression than Japanese men and women. Given the measure of depression that lacks cultural equivalence between Japanese and Americans (*see* Table 6.7), one should not conclude that both American men and women are more depressed than Japanese men and women. In addition, although the correlation of age and depression is greater in the American data than in the Japanese data, it is not meaningful to conclude that the age has a stronger effect on depression among Americans than Japanese because the measure of depression has no cross-cultural equivalence.

The examples provided throughout this chapter offer social work researchers some descriptive statistical techniques for cross-cultural evaluation of measurement equivalence. These descriptive statistical analyses are useful but do not provide researchers with definitive answers to the issues of cross-cultural equivalence in the measurement properties of the research instruments or outcome measures. When there are limitations in the data and sample sizes, these descriptive statistical techniques are sufficient to give researchers meaningful guidance in the assessment of cross-cultural equivalence in the research instruments.

Chapter 7 will explain and illustrate the process and procedures of testing cross-cultural equivalence hypotheses concerning the measurement properties of the research instruments across cultural groups. This is the crucial stage in the process of cross-cultural instrument development.

7

Testing Cross-Cultural Measurement Invariance

LISREL Applications

T his chapter will provide extensive examples and illustrations of the applications of LISREL confirmatory factor analysis (CFA) and multisample CFA in the testing of the cross-cultural equivalence of measurement properties.

Confirmatory Factor Analysis

Both exploratory factor analysis (EFA) and CFA can be used to evaluate the factor structure of a set of observed items in terms of their relationship with their respective factors or latent constructs. More specifically, both EFA and CFA focus on the relationship between observed items of a scale or index and their underlying latent factors or constructs. This relationship indicates how well an abstract concept is measured by its observed items or indicators. Therefore, the strength and magnitude of the "factor loadings" are of primary purpose (Byrne, 1998). Among other things, the key difference between EFA and CFA is that EFA does not specify which observed items belong to which factor in advance as CFA does. In an EFA analysis, all selected observed items are assumed to load on all possible factors or latent constructs. The researchers do not specify the relationships between observed items and latent constructs in advance. In Chapter 6, the equivalence comparisons of the factor structures were not based on any tests of significance. At best, researchers can only eyeball the values of the factor loadings and the factor pattern between the comparative groups and speculate some degree of equivalency based on what the data show.

Confirmatory factor analysis via LISREL or other structural equation modeling software, such as AMOS and EQS or MPLUS (Byrne, 2001, 1995; Raykov & Marcoulodes, 2006), can be used to test different types of hypotheses concerning the measurement properties of a scale or index, especially hypotheses concerning cross-cultural equivalence of a research instrument.

There has been a general consensus that multigroup (sample) CFA offers a strong approach to evaluate cross-cultural equivalence of measurement properties (Jan-Benedict & Baumgartner, 1998). Researchers have proposed different procedural steps in the testing of measurement equivalence hypotheses, including the equivalence of the covariance matrices of the observed indicators and the equivalence of factor means among groups (Vandenberg & Lance, 2000). This chapter will illustrate the steps of testing the measurement equivalence or testing the invariance of the factor structure across groups as suggested by Joreskog and Sorbom (2001) using LISREL 8.7. They recommended the testing of five general hypotheses as follows:

Ho. A. Testing the hypothesis of equivalence of covariance matrices of observed indicators of a scale or an instrument between comparative groups

Ho. B. Testing the hypothesis of equivalence of factor patterns of observed indicators across groups

Ho. C. Testing the hypothesis of equivalence of factor loadings of observed indicators on their respective factors across groups

Ho. D. Testing the hypothesis of equivalence of measurement errors of observed indicators across groups

Ho. E. Testing the hypothesis of equivalence of factor variances and covariance across groups

It is rare that one can find an absolute equivalence of all measurement properties across the comparative groups. Jan-Benedict and Baumgartner (1988) suggested that invariance of factor pattern and factor loadings are sufficient to determine whether a construct can be measured across different cultural, national, or racial groups. However, if the purpose is to compare the latent means of a construct across groups, then one needs to establish both metric equivalence (same-factor loadings) and scalar invariance (same-item intercepts). This chapter emphasizes the importance of having equivalence of factor pattern and factor loadings as the fundamental steps in the construction of a cross-cultural research instrument (Hoelter, 1983). In addition, equivalence of factor pattern and factor loadings is sufficient to compare the relationships among the variables under some theoretical assumptions. For example, if a researcher plans to investigate whether social support associates with life satisfaction in two different racial elderly populations, it is important for the researcher to use the social support scale and the life satisfaction scale that have similar factor pattern and factor loadings between these two populations.

Basic Components of a LISREL Confirmatory Factor Analysis Model

There are some basic LISREL command file symbols and notations that are important to understand to perform and interpret LISREL analysis. Explanations and interpretations of these symbols and notations are discussed throughout the examples. There are two LISREL measurement models, as illustrated in the following equations.

Measurement Model for Observed X variables:

$$X = \Lambda_X \xi + \delta$$

Measurement Model for Observed Y variables:

$$Y = \Lambda_y \eta + \varepsilon$$

In the aforementioned equations, X and Y are observed variables of selected latent constructs. Λ_X (Lambda X) and Λ_y (Lambda Y) are factor loadings of X and Y variables on their respective latent variables. ξ (Ksi) and η (Eta) are latent variables of X and Y. δ (Delta) and ε (Epsilon) are measurement errors of X and Y variables.

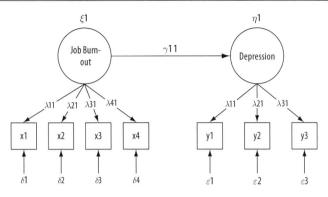

Figure 7.1 Job Burn-out and Depression

Assumptions

There are three basic assumptions for a measurement model.

1. The measurement errors (δ) of observed variables X are uncorrelated with the latent variable (ξ).
2. The measurement errors (ε of observed variables Y's are uncorrelated with the latent variable (η).
3. The measurement errors (δ) of observed variables, X, are uncorrelated with the measurement errors (ε) of observed variables, Y.

Let's assume that a researcher hypothesizes that job burnout is a risk factor of depression among social workers (see Figure 7.1). Job burnout is measured by a scale of four items and depression by a scale of three items. The following structural equation model illustrates the causal relationships between job burnout and depression and the respective LISREL notations expressed in the aforementioned equations.

$\xi 1$ is the latent variable of job burnout.
X1 to X4 are four observed items of job burnout.
$\lambda 1$ to $\lambda 4$ are the relationships (factor loadings) between job burnout and its four observed indicators.
$\delta 1$ to $\delta 4$ are the measurement errors of observed items, X.
$\eta 1$ is the latent variable of depression.
Y1 to Y3 are three observed items of depression.

λ.1 to λ.3 are the relationships (factor loadings) between depression and its three observed indicators.

ε1 to ε3 are the measurement of observed items, Y.

γ11 (gamma) is the path coefficient of depression on job burnout.

Preparing Input Data for LISREL Analysis

Correlations and covariances of the observed variables are commonly used as input data for LISREL. There are different ways to generate correlation and covariance matrices of observed variables for LISREL analysis. LISREL's companion software PRELIS 2 can be used to generate different types of correlations and covariances. Specifically, one can use PRELIS 2 to generate *(a)* a polychromic correlation matrix of ordinal variables; *(b)* a polyserial correlation matrix of ordinal and continuous variables; *(c)* a Pearson correlation matrix; and *(d)* an augmented moment matrix. Researchers often use either a Pearson correlation matrix or a covariance matrix as input data for LISREL analysis. These two types of matrix can be generated by any statistical software, including SAS and SPSS. In this book SPSS is used to generate data for LISREL analyses.

Preparing Data via SPSS

There are a few rules that data analysts should always follow in preparing data for a cross-cultural analysis.

1. **Reviewing and Verifying Data**. Data analysts should begin the process of data analysis with a careful review and verification of the coding of the measurement items across groups. All items of a scale or index should be coded the same across the comparative groups. Using the DESCRIPTIVES procedure of SPSS, one can generate the information concerning descriptive statistics for each item of a scale or an instrument.

2. **Missing Data**. Analysts should check for missing data in each item. Missing data in any item of a scale will reduce the sample size. If missing data is a concern, then analysts can use different methods of missing data treatments to handle the data as suggested in the literature (Kim & Curry, 1977; Litlle & Rubin, 1987; McDonald, Thurton, & Nelson, 2000). Treatment of missing data is beyond the scope of this book.

3. **Direction of Correlations**. Correlation of the items of a scale should be positive. All items of a scale should correlate in the same direction. If there is a negative correlation between any items, then analysts should verify the coding of these items to correct the problem.

Performing Exploratory Factor Analysis

Once the data are checked, cleaned, and verified, analyst can perform an EFA to identify the underlying dimensions or factors of the observed items. Examples of EFA were provided in the previous chapter. In using the SPSS' DATA REDUCTION Procedure for factor analysis, analysts should select the Descriptive command to generate coefficients and significance levels for the correlation matrix, this information is useful for the initial screening of the quality of the items of a scale. Items that have poor correlation should be excluded from the analysis; under the EXTRACTION command, analysts should select PRINCIPAL AXIS FACTORING or MAXIMUM LIKELIHOOD if the sample is large. Under the ROTATION command, VARIMAX is the choice because this procedure will generate independent factors underlying the observed items. The key result that analysts should pay attention to is the ROTATED FACTOR MATRIX. Factor loadings should range between 0.30 and 1.00.

Literature Review and Expert Opinions

Naming and defining the factors generated from EFA can sometimes be difficult and confused. Reviewing the related literature can provide researchers useful insight in naming and defining the factors underlying the observed items. In addition, consulting with experts in the field will also help researchers interpret the meanings of the factors.

Generating Correlation and Covariance Matrices

Once the dimensions or factor structures are identified in each comparative group, analysts can begin to generate input data for CFA via LISREL. Both correlation matrices and covariance matrices can be generated using different statistical procedures in SPSS.

Generating Correlation Matrices via Regression Procedure

Under the REGRESSION procedure, analysts can generate the correlation matrix for LISREL input using the LINEAR command. One of the items has to be listed as the dependent variable and the remaining variables as independent variables. Once the dependent variable and independent variables are selected, to generate the correlation matrix for these variables, analysts should "click" on the STATISTICS box and select the CORRELATION command, then "run" the analysis.

Generating Correlation Matrices and Covariance Matrices via the SCALE Procedure

Under the SCALE procedure, analysts use the RELIABILITY ANALYSIS to generate the correlation and covariance matrices. Once the items or variables are selected, analysts choose the STATISTICS command and select the commands CORRELATIONS and COVARIANCES of the INTER-ITEM procedures.

Generating Correlation Matrices via the DATA REDUCTION Procedure

Under this procedure, analysts use the FACTOR command to generate a correlation matrix by selecting the command COEFFICIENTS. Similarly to the REGRESSION procedure, the FACTOR procedure allows analysts three options for the treatment of missing data.

The correlation or covariance matrices can be typed directly into the LISREL syntax command file. Analysts can also use data-editing programs like NotePad to create a data file for LISREL. **Notepad** is a free source code editor running under the MS Windows environment (see http://notepad-plus.sourceforge.net/uk/site.htm).

LISREL Confirmatory Factor Analysis

As mentioned earlier, nine items of the Center for Epidemiologic Studies Depression Scale (Radloff, 1977, 1991) were selected from the American's Changing Lives data set for examples of LISREL CFA and cross-cultural equivalence analyses of the research instruments (House, 2006).

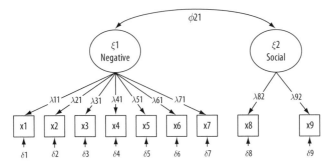

Figure 7.2 Confirmatory Factor Analysis of Nine CESD Items

In the previous section, EFA analyses were performed on these nine CESD items for both older African-Americans and Whites ages 60 years and older using the American's Changing Lives Survey (House, 2006). The diagram in Figure 7.2 illustrates the measurement model of these items in a CFA.

Covariance matrices are used as input data for the following LISREL CFAs. In this example, the covariance matrices are manually entered in the LISREL syntax only file. LISREL 8.7 (Joreskog & Sorbom, 2004) is used here.

The CFA diagram in Figure 7.2 has the following information:

1. The measurement model has two latent constructs (factors): negative feelings (Negative) and social relationship problem (Social). These two latent constructs are presented in the two circles.

2. The negative feelings construct has seven items, and the social relationship problem has two items, as indicated in previous EFAs. The observed indicators of the two latent constructs are presented in the squared boxes. The arrows from the latent constructs to their respective observed items indicate that they are "reflective indicators" (Edwards & Bagozzi, 2000; Bollen 1989). Specifically, the latent constructs are the causes of the observed indicators. The factor loadings indicate the causal relationships between a latent construct and its respective observed indicators or items.

3. Each observed indicator in the model also has an error term. The error terms are the causes of the observed indicators. If the latent constructs have perfect causal relationships with their respective observed items, the error terms would be zero.

The following LISREL 8.7 Command File 1 is a simple CFA.

Command File 1.
```
CFA 9 CESD ITEMS TWO FACTOR MODEL OLDER BLACK
DA NI=9 NO=471
CM
.411
.195 .535
.170 .178 .502
.202 .175 .182 .429
.138 .124 .171 .172 .463
.209 .168 .155 .231 .140 .382
.190 .224 .185 .185 .138 .198 .469
.088 .062 .079 .091 .055 .089 .084 .286
.078 .067 .082 .088 .070 .105 .086 .155 .223
LA
DEPRESS EFFORT SLEEP LONELY EATING SAD GOING UNFRIEND DISLIKE
MO NX=9 NK=2
LK
NEGATIVE SOCIAL
FR LX 2 1 LX 3 1 LX 4 1 LX 5 1 LX 6 1 LX 7 1 LX 9 2
VALUE 1 LX 1 1 LX 8 2
OU SE SC TV
```

In Command File 1, the first line is the title, "CFA 9 CESD ITEMS TWO FACTOR MODEL OLDER BLACK." Analysts are free to use titles that are easy to remember and related to the goal of an analysis.

The second line of Command File 1 is the DATA specifications of the analysis, "DA NI = 9 NO = 471." The NI = 9 specification indicates that there are nine input variables in the input data. The NO = 471 specification indicates that the sample size of this analysis is 471.

The third line is for input data. Two common input matrices are correlation and covariance matrices. The letters "KM" represent the correlation matrix and "CM" represent the covariance matrix. If a correlation matrix is used, then analysts should include the means and standard deviations of the items used in the analysis. In this example, the covariance matrix of the nine CESD items is used as input data for the analysis.

Following the CM specification is the input matrix. There is no need to enter the full matrix. It is important to enter the correlation or covariance coefficients carefully.

The LA line is the specification of the labels of the observed items. The line after the LA line is the list of the names of the observed items included in the covariance matrix. The label of each observed item should be restricted to no more than eight characters. There are nine labels representing the nine observed items in the covariance matrix. Again, the labels should be meaningful and related to the contents of the items.

The MO line is the CFA model specification. The notation "NX = 9" specifies that there are nine observed variables in the CFA model. The notation "NK = 2" specifies that there are two latent constructs or factors in this CFA model.

The LK line is the specification of the labels of the latent constructs. The procedure of naming the labels for the latent constructs is the same as those of the observed items. These labels should be meaningful and easily recognized.

The line after the LK line is the list of the names or labels of the latent constructs. In this example, NEGATIVE is used to refer to the seven items that are assumed to measure negative feelings and SOCIAL refers to the two items that are assumed to measure social relationship problem. Again, the labels should be restricted to no more than eight characters.

The FR line is the specification of the factor loading estimates of the observed items on their respective latent constructs. Note that in an EFA the analyst has no means to specify which observed item should be loaded on which factor. In a CFA, analysts can specify in advance the relationships between observed items and their latent constructs. For example, FR LX 2 1 refers to the specification of the relationship between item 2 ("I felt everything I did was an effort") and the latent construct 1 (NEGATIVE: negative feelings).

The VA line is the specification of the scaling and identification for the latent variables (Byrne, 1998). By convention, the first item of each latent construct is assigned the value of one. In this CFA model, VA 1 LX 1 1 and LX 8 2 indicate that the first observed item of the latent construct 1 is assigned a value of 1, and the first observed item ("People were unfriendly") of the latent construct 2 (SOCIAL: social relationship problem) is also assigned a value of 1.

The OU line is the specification for the expected outputs of the analysis. In this example, the command file is expected to produce the standard errors for the estimates (SEs), the completed standardized solutions for the estimates (SCs), and the t-values as test of statistical significance for the estimates (TVs). There are other options for outputs in LISREL; analysts can decide on which results they want to generate and specify them appropriately.

The LISREL CFA Command File for the sample older Whites is the same as the command file of the sample of older African-Americans with the exception of the title line, sample size (NO), and the values of the covariance coefficients (*see* http://www.oup.com/us for the complete command file).

Running LISREL WINDOW APPLICATION

Command File 1 can be entered directly to the LISREL WINDOW APPLICATION. Once the LISREL program is activated, analysts can select the FILE menu and choose the NEW command that will appear on the screen and begin to enter the command file. Once the typing is completed, analysts should save it then go to the RUN menu to run the analysis. There are two RUN icons, one for LISREL and one for PRELIS. For all examples in this book, Run LISREL is the choice. The program executes the input file quickly, and the results are instantly presented on the computer screen. Command Files 1 and 2 (see p. 100) should be executed separately.

Following are the few samples of the results from the LISREL analyses.

DATE: 2/16/2007
TIME: 23:16
L I S R E L 8.71
BY
Karl G. Joreskog & Dag Sorbom
This program is published exclusively by
Scientific Software International, Inc.
7383 N. Lincoln Avenue, Suite 100
Lincolnwood, IL 60712, U.S.A.
Phone: (800)247-6113, (847)675-0720, Fax: (847)675-2140

The following lines were read from file C:\Program Files\SPSS\BLACK_ CFA_9CESD_ITEMS.LS8:

The line Files\SPSS\BLACK_CFA_9CESD_ITEMS.LS8 indicates where the input program was stored on the analyst's computer (\SPSS\) and the name of the input program (BLACK_CFA_9CESD_ITEMS.LS8). After the Files line, the program reports the original input program and the following specifications.

Number of Input Variables 9
Number of Y - Variables 0
Number of X - Variables 9
Number of ETA - Variables 0
Number of KSI - Variables 2
Number of Observations 471

The aforementioned information verifies and confirms the input program. Note that in the DA line, the command file specifies the number of input variables as $NI = 9$. No Y variables were declared, and the number of X variables is nine. No endogenous ETA latent variables were declared. The command file specifies two KSI latent variables, and the sample size (number of observations) is 471.

Parameter Specifications
LAMBDA-X

	NEGATIVE	SOCIAL
DEPRESS	0	0
EFFORT	1	0
SLEEP	2	0
LONELY	3	0
EATING	4	0
SAD	5	0
GOING	6	0
UNFRIEND	0	0
DISLIKE	0	7

The above matrix indicates that the program will estimate seven LAMBDA X (factor loadings). The first item of NEGATIVE and SOCIAL was fixed with a value of 1 for the scaling purpose for the two latent variables.

PHI

	NEGATIVE	SOCIAL
NEGATIVE	8	
SOCIAL	9	10

PHI is the variance and covariance matrix of the latent constructs. The aforementioned matrix indicates that after the command file estimates 7 LAMBDA X parameters; the following parameters 8, 9, and 10 are variance and covariance estimates of the two latent variables.

THETA-DELTA

DEPRESS	EFFORT	SLEEP	LONELY	EATING	SAD
11	12	13	14	15	16

THETA-DELTA

GOING	UNFRIEND	DISLIKE
17	18	19

THETA-DELTA coefficients are the parameters of error measurements of the observed items. These parameters of error measurement are reported after the estimation of the factor loadings, the variances, and covariance of the latent constructs.

LISREL Estimates (Maximum Likelihood)
LAMBDA-X (*Unstandardized Factor Loadings*)

	NEGATIVE	SOCIAL
DEPRESS	1.00	
EFFORT	0.93	
	(0.09)	
	10.70	
SLEEP	0.89	
	(0.08)	
	10.63	

LONELY	1.06	
	(0.08)	
	13.20	
EATING	0.76	
	(0.08)	
	9.46	
SAD	1.04	
	(0.08)	
	13.61	
GOING	0.99	
	(0.08)	
	12.04	
UNFRIEND		1.00
DISLIKE		1.04
		(0.12)
		8.54

PHI (*Variances and Covariances*)

	NEGATIVE	SOCIAL
NEGATIVE	0.19	
	(0.02)	
	7.88	
SOCIAL	0.08	0.15
	(0.01)	(0.02)
	6.34	6.48

THETA-DELTA (*Measurement Errors of Observed Items*)

DEPRESS	EFFORT	SLEEP	LONELY	EATING	SAD
0.22	0.37	0.35	0.21	0.35	0.17
(0.02)	(0.03)	(0.02)	(0.02)	(0.02)	(0.01)
12.67	13.99	14.02	12.29	14.40	11.76

THETA-DELTA

GOING	UNFRIEND	DISLIKE
0.28	0.14	0.06
(0.02)	(0.02)	(0.02)
13.30	7.48	3.42

These results include three important types of information: the factor loadings or causal relationships between the latent constructs and their respective observed items, the variances and covariances of the latent constructs, and the measurement errors of the observed items. Under the matrix of LAMBDA X, the command file produces unstandardized factor loadings, the SEs enclosed in the parentheses, and the t-values as the test statistical significance for the estimates. One can test the hypothesis that a particular observed item has a statistically significant relationship with its respective latent construct. Note that the first observed item of both latent constructs has a value of 1. This value will be estimated in the standardized solutions. Let's look at the factor loading of the item "I felt that everything I did was an **effort**" on its latent construct of NEGATIVE or negative feelings. This item has an unstandardized factor loading of 0.90, a SE of 0.09, and a t-value of 10.70. The t-value is the ratio of the factor loading over its SE (0.90/0.09 = 10.33). The t-value in the parenthesis is slightly different from the output because of the rounding values. The LISREL output does not produce an exact level of significance for the values. However, by convention, a t-value of 2.00 or greater is significant at 0.05 or smaller. The results of the PHI (variance and covariance) and the results of THETA-DELTA (measurement errors of observed items) are interpreted similarly.

Goodness-of-Fit Statistics

Although LISREL analysis offers more than three dozen measures of fit, only a few have meaningful application for the interpretation of how well the model fits the data.

Degrees of Freedom = 26
Minimum Fit Function Chi-Square = 49.24 ($p = 0.0039$)

Root mean square error of approximation (RMSEA) = 0.044
90% confidence interval for RMSEA = (0.025; 0.062)
p-Value for test of close fit (RMSEA < 0.05) = 0.68

Non-Normed fit index (NNFI) = 0.98
Comparative fit index (CFI) = 0.99

Standardized RMR = 0.030
Goodness-of-fit index (GFI) = 0.98
Adjusted goodness-of-fit index (AGFI) = 0.96

Byrne (1998) presented a thoughtful discussion on the utility of the goodness of fit. Among these were the minimum fit function chi-square; this test should have a probability value greater than 0.05 for the model to fit the data well. However, this test is sensitive to sample size; therefore, it is recommended that researchers should use additional measures of fit in assessing the fit of a model. Following are some additional recommended measures of fit:

1. RMSEA: The value should be less than 0.05 and no greater than 0.08 (Vanderberg & Lance, 2000).
2. Standardized root-mean-square residual (SRMSR): The value should be at 0.08 or less and no greater than 0.10 (Vanderberg & Lance, 2000).
3. NNFI or Tucker-Lewis index (TLI): The value should be equal to or greater than 0.90 and closer to or equal 1.00 (Jan-Benedict & Baumgartner, 1998)
4. CFI: The value should be greater than 0.90 and closer to or equal 1.00 (Jan-Benedict & Baumgartner, 1998).
5. The GFI and AGFI should have the value from 0.90 and closer to 1.00.

In reviewing the results of goodness-of-fit for the African-American sample, the minimum fit function chi-square with 26 degrees of freedom is 49.24 ($p = 0.0039$). This suggests that the CFA model does not fit the data well. However, all other GFIs indicate that the CFA model does fit the data very well. The RMSEA has a value of 0.04. The SRMSR has a value of 0.03. The NNFI is 0.98. The CFI is 0.99. The GFI and AGFI have values of 0.98 and 0.96, respectively. These measures of fit indicate that the CFA model of nine items and two latent factors fits very well with the data for African-Americans Blacks.

LISREL Results for Whites

Note that the model specifications of the CFA model of the nine CESD items are the same for both African-Americans and Whites. In the following, only the essential results are presented for Whites.

LISREL Estimates (Maximum Likelihood)
LAMBDA-X (*Unstandardized Factor Loadings*)

	NEGATIVE	SOCIAL
DEPRESSE	1.00	
EFFORT	0.85	
	(0.05)	
	16.74	

SLEEP	0.67	
	(0.05)	
	12.33	
LONELY	0.86	
	(0.05)	
	18.77	
EATING	0.58	
	(0.04)	
	12.91	
SAD	0.90	
	(0.04)	
	19.94	
GOING	0.73	
	(0.05)	
	15.46	
UNFRIEND		1.00
DISLIKE		0.92
		(0.10)
		9.09

PHI

	NEGATIVE	SOCIAL
	-------	-----
NEGATIVE	0.19	
	(0.01)	
	13.26	
SOCIAL	0.06	0.07
	(0.01)	(0.01)
	9.11	7.06

THETA-DELTA (Measurement Errors of Observed Items)

DEPRESSE	EFFORT	SLEEP	LONELY	EATING	SAD
0.14	0.29	0.41	0.20	0.27	0.17
(0.01)	(0.01)	(0.02)	(0.01)	(0.01)	(0.01)
16.06	20.89	22.32	19.68	22.18	18.64

THETA-DELTA

GOING	UNFRIENDLY	DISLIKE
0.27	0.12	0.08

(0.01)   (0.01)   (0.01)
21.42   13.83   11.67

Goodness-of-Fit Statistics

The following selected measures of fit are extracted from the results of the LISREL output. The full list of goodness-of-fit statistics were presented previously, therefore there is no need to report them again.

Degrees of Freedom $= 26$
Minimum Fit Function Chi-Square $= 142.03\ (p = 0.0)$
RMSEA $= 0.065$
Standardized RMR $= 0.037$
NNFI $= 0.95$
CFI $= 0.97$
GFI $= 0.97$
AGFI $= 0.95$

Similarly to the goodness-of-fit statistics in the African-American sample, the minimum fit function chi-square with 26 degrees of freedom has a value of 142.03 and its associated p-value is 0.000, indicating the CFA model does not fit the data well. The RMSEA has a value of 0.06. The SRMR is 0.03. The NNFI is 0.95. The CFI is 0.97. The GFI is 0.97, and the AGFI is 0.95. These measures of fit also confirm that the CFA model fits the data of the Whites well. In comparing these measures of goodness-of-fit statistics between the African-Americans and Whites, it appears that the CFA model has a better fit with the data among African-Americans than among Whites.

Assessing Equivalence of Factor Structures: Measurement Invariance

Once the initial factor structure of the scale is established via EFA and CFA for each of the comparative groups, the next step is to evaluate the factor structures of that scale or instrument across groups. Joreskog and Sorbom (2001) suggested five psychometric elements that needed to be tested between groups: *(1)* the covariance matrices of the observed items; *(2)* the factor pattern of the observed items; *(3)* the factor loadings of the observed items; *(4)* the measurement errors of the observed items; and *(5)* the variances and covariances of the latent constructs or factors. Among these elements, the second and third elements are important for the establishment of conceptual and metric equivalence, which are fundamental to cross-cultural comparisons.

Following are examples of how to test five basic hypotheses concerning the equivalence of factor structure in cross-cultural research. For each hypothesis, there is an example of a LISREL command file and relevant results.

Ho. A. Nine selected items of the CESD scale exhibit an equivalence of covariance structures between older African-Americans and older Whites. The test of Ho. A is considered as the omnibus test (Vanderberg, 2002). This hypothesis rarely is supported. If it were supported, then all assumptions of measurement equivalence across groups are supported. However, when it is rejected, it does not mean that all other assumptions of equivalence of the measurement properties are also rejected. Some researchers have ignored this test in their analyses of measurement invariances (Deng, Doll, Hendrickson, & Scazzero, 2005; Anderson, Hughes, Fisher, & Nicklas, 2005).

Command File 2
EQUIVALENCE OF COVARIANCE STRUCTURES: HO. A
GROUP 1: OLDER BLACK
DA NI=9 NO=471 NG=2
CM
.411
.195 .535
.170 .178 .502
.202 .175 .182 .429
.138 .124 .171 .172 .463
.209 .168 .155 .231 .140 .382
.190 .224 .185 .185 .138 .198 .469
.088 .062 .079 .091 .055 .089 .084 .286
.078 .067 .082 .088 .070 .105 .086 .155 .223
LA
DEPRESS EFFORT SLEEP LONELY EATING SAD GOING UNFRIEND DISLIKE
MO NX=9 NK=9 LX=ID TD=ZE
OU
GROUP 2: OLDER WHITE

EQUIVALENCE OF COVARIANCE STRUCTURES: HO. A
DA NI=9 NO=1099
CM
.328
.166 .425
.119 .098 .492
.167 .119 .103 .345
.100 .125 .081 .085 .332
.177 .115 .111 .161 .085 .325
.124 .160 .128 .102 .093 .113 .373
.058 .049 .038 .067 .050 .053 .038 .192
.051 .053 .036 .046 .026 .059 .051 .062 .139
LA
DEPRESS EFFORT SLEEP LONELY EATING SAD GOING UNFRIEND DISLIKE
MO PH=IN
OU

In this LISREL input command file, the MO line specifies that there are nine observed items (NX = 9), each observed item represents one latent variable (NK = 9).

The main purpose of this analysis is to test the hypothesis that the covariance structures of the nine items of the CESD are the same between the two comparative groups. The only test of significance statistics that researchers should note is the **minimum fit function chi-square**, which is the test of significance that allows analysts to make their decision on rejecting the hypothesis or not rejecting it (Joreskog & Sorbom, 2001). If this test fails to reject Hypothesis A, then all elements of the factor structures of the scale, including factor pattern, loadings, and error variance, are invariant or equivalent between the comparative groups. If Hypothesis A is rejected, then four more hypotheses should be tested.

In the LISREL outputs, there are two types of goodness-of-fit statistics: group goodness-of-fit statistics and global goodness of fit. Each comparative group has its own goodness-of-fit statistics. The key statistic that analysts use to reject or fail to reject the hypothesis of interest is the **minimum fit function chi-square** reported under the global goodness of fit. This chi-square test must have a probability value greater than 0.05 ($p > .05$) for the analysts to draw a conclusion that there is cross-cultural equivalence in all elements of the factor structures of a scale.

All other measures of goodness-of-fit statistics are for information only (Joreskog & Sorbom, 2001).

Goodness of Fit Statistics for African-Americans
Group Goodness of Fit Statistics
Contribution to Chi-Square = 105.60
Percentage Contribution to Chi-Square = 63.07
RMR = 0.044
Standardized RMR = 0.14
GFI = 0.95

Goodness of Fit Statistics for Equivalence Hypothesis
Global Goodness of Fit Statistics

Degrees of Freedom = 45
Minimum Fit Function Chi-Square = 167.45 (**$p = 0.00$**)

RMSEA = 0.063
90 Percent Confidence Interval for RMSEA = (0.054 ; 0.072)
P-Value for Test of Close Fit (RMSEA < 0.05) = 0.012
CFI = 0.98

Goodness of Fit Statistics for Whites
Group Goodness of Fit Statistics
Contribution to Chi-Square = 61.84
Percentage Contribution to Chi-Square = 36.93
RMR = 0.019
Standardized RMR = 0.060
GFI = 0.99

The results confirm that Ho. A. "Nine selected items of the CESD scale exhibit an equivalence of covariance structures between older Blacks and older Whites" is rejected given that the value of the chi-square and its associated probability value is less than 0.05; the next hypothesis will be tested.

Ho. B. Nine selected items of the CESD scale exhibit an equivalence of factor pattern between older Blacks and older Whites.

More specifically, nine CESD items are hypothesized to hold two factors or two latent constructs with the negative factor having seven items and social factor having two items. This hypothesis will be used as the baseline hypothesis (baseline model) for the comparison with the next hypothesis of equal factor loadings as the subsequent hypothesis is nested in this hypothesis (Anderson, Hughes, Fisher, & Nicklas, 2005). The above hypothesis will be tested in the following LISREL command file.

Command File 3
```
EQUIVALENCE OF FACTOR PATTERN: HO B
GROUP 1: OLDER BLACK
DA NI=9 NO=471 NG=2
CM
.411
.195 .535
.170 .178 .502
.202 .175 .182 .429
.138 .124 .171 .172 .463
.209 .168 .155 .231 .140 .382
.190 .224 .185 .185 .138 .198 .469
.088 .062 .079 .091 .055 .089 .084 .286
.078 .067 .082 .088 .070 .105 .086 .155 .223
LA
DEPRESS EFFORT SLEEP LONELY EATING SAD GOING UNFRIEND DISLIKE
MO NX=9 NK=2
LK
NEGATIVE SOCIAL
FR LX 2 1 LX 3 1 LX 4 1 LX 5 1 LX 6 1 LX 7 1 LX 9 2
VALUE 1 LX 1 1 LX 8 2
OU
EQUIVALENCE OF FACTOR PATTERN: HO B
GROUP 2: OLDER WHITE
DA NI=9 NO=1099
CM
.328
.166 .425
.119 .098 .492
.167 .119 .103 .345
.100 .125 .081 .085 .332
.177 .115 .111 .161 .085 .325
.124 .160 .128 .102 .093 .113 .373
.058 .049 .038 .067 .050 .053 .038 .192
.051 .053 .036 .046 .026 .059 .051 .062 .139
LA
DEPRESS EFFORT SLEEP LONELY EATING SAD GOING UNFRIEND DISLIKE
MO LX=PS
```

LK
NEGATIVE SOCIAL
OU

Note that the differences in command file 3 and command file 2 that tested Ho. A are in the MO Line of Group 1 (African-Americans) and the MO line of Group 2 (Whites). The command file specifies that nine observed items (NK = 9) have two factors or latent constructs (NK = 2); items 2, 3, 4, 5, 6, and 7 belong to factor 1 and they are considered to be free parameters and will be estimated (FR LX 2 1 LX 3 1 LX 4 1 LX 5 1 LX 6 1 LX 7 1 LX 9 2). The specification of LX 1 1 can be read as "item 1 belongs to factor 1," and so on. Similarly, LX 9 2 can be read as "item 9 belongs to factor 2." The VALUE line specifies that items 1 and 8 are considered to be fixed at the value of 1.

In the MO line of group 2 (Whites), the command file specifies that all nine observed item (LX) have the same pattern and the same starting values as those in group 1 (LX = PS).

Here are the results of goodness-of-fit statistics:

Group Goodness of Fit Statistics (African-Americans)
Contribution to Chi-Square = 49.24
Percentage Contribution to Chi-Square = 25.74

RMR = 0.013
Standardized RMR = 0.030
GFI = 0.98

Global Goodness of Fit Statistics
Degrees of Freedom = 52
Minimum Fit Function Chi-Square = 191.27 (P = 0.0)

RMSEA = 0.060
90% Confidence Interval for RMSEA = (0.051 ; 0.069)
p-Value for Test of Close Fit (RMSEA < 0.05) = 0.036
NNFI = 0.97
CFI = 0.97

Group Goodness of Fit Statistics (Whites)
Contribution to Chi-Square = 142.03
Percentage Contribution to Chi-Square = 74.26

Root Mean Square Residual (RMR) = 0.013
Standardized RMR = 0.037
GFI = 0.97

The selection and interpretation of the measures of goodness of fit concerning the testing of the nested hypothesis involving different levels of factor structure invariance will be presented in Table 7.1.

The following LISREL command file is for the testing of Ho. C.

Ho. C. The factor loadings of nine observed indicators are equivalent between African-Americans and Whites.

The difference between command file 4 and command file 3 is in the MO line of Group 2 (Whites). In the Command file 3, LX was specified as LX = PS (same pattern), but in command file 4, LX is specified as LX = IN (invariant).

Command File 4

```
EQUIVALENCE OF FACTOR LOADINGS: HO. C
GROUP 1: OLDER BLACK
DA NI=9 NO=471 NG=2
CM
.411
.195 .535
.170 .178 .502
.202 .175 .182 .429
.138 .124 .171 .172 .463
.209 .168 .155 .231 .140 .382
.190 .224 .185 .185 .138 .198 .469
.088 .062 .079 .091 .055 .089 .084 .286
.078 .067 .082 .088 .070 .105 .086 .155 .223
LA
DEPRESS EFFORT SLEEP LONELY EATING SAD GOING UNFRIEND DISLIKE
MO NX=9 NK=2
LK
NEGATIVE SOCIAL
FR LX 2 1 LX 3 1 LX 4 1 LX 5 1 LX 6 1 LX 7 1 LX 9 2
VALUE 1 LX 1 1 LX 8 2
OU
EQUIVALENCE OF FACTOR LOADINGS: HO. C
GROUP 2: OLDER WHITE
DA NI=9 NO=1099
CM
.328
.166 .425
.119 .098 .492
```

.167 .119 .103 .345
.100 .125 .081 .085 .332
.177 .115 .111 .161 .085 .325
.124 .160 .128 .102 .093 .113 .373
.058 .049 .038 .067 .050 .053 .038 .192
.051 .053 .036 .046 .026 .059 .051 .062 .139
LA
DEPRESS EFFORT SLEEP LONELY EATING SAD GOING UNFRIEND DISLIKE
MO LX=IN
LK
NEGATIVE SOCIAL
OU

The summary results of the Goodness of Fit Tests for Ho. C are:

Group Goodness of Fit Statistics (African-Americans)
Contribution to Chi-Square = 57.68
Percentage Contribution to Chi-Square = 28.20

RMR = 0.020
Standardized RMR = 0.044
GFI = 0.97

Global Goodness of Fit Statistics
Degrees of Freedom = 59
Minimum Fit Function Chi-Square = 204.54 (**$p = 0.0$**)

RMSEA = 0.057
90% Confidence Interval for RMSEA = (0.049 ; 0.066)
p-Value for Test of Close Fit (RMSEA < 0.05) = 0.073

NNFI = 0.97
CFI = 0.97

Group Goodness of Fit Statistics (Whites)
Contribution to Chi-Square = 146.86
Percentage Contribution to Chi-Square = 71.80

RMR = 0.014
Standardized RMR = 0.038
GFI = 0.97

The next hypothesis to be tested is Ho. D.

Ho. D. The measurement errors of nine CESD items are equivalent between Blacks and Whites.

This hypothesis postulates that the Theta-Delta or measurement error estimates of the observed indicators are the same between African-Americans and Whites. This hypothesis is tested by the following the LISREL command file.

Command File 5

```
FACTORIAL EQUIVALENCE CFA 9 CESD ITEMS: HO D
GROUP 1: OLDER BLACK
DA NI=9 NO=471 NG=2
CM
.411
.195 .535
.170 .178 .502
.202 .175 .182 .429
.138 .124 .171 .172 .463
.209 .168 .155 .231 .140 .382
.190 .224 .185 .185 .138 .198 .469
.088 .062 .079 .091 .055 .089 .084 .286
.078 .067 .082 .088 .070 .105 .086 .155 .223
LA
DEPRESS EFFORT SLEEP LONELY EATING SAD GOING UNFRIEND DISLIKE
MO NX=9 NK=2
LK
NEGATIVE SOCIAL
FR LX 2 1 LX 3 1 LX 4 1 LX 5 1 LX 6 1 LX 7 1 LX 9 2
VALUE 1 LX 1 1 LX 8 2
OU
CFA 9 CESD ITEMS TWO FACTOR MODEL OLDER WHITE
DA NI=9 NO=1099
CM
.328
.166 .425
.119 .098 .492
.167 .119 .103 .345
.100 .125 .081 .085 .332
.177 .115 .111 .161 .085 .325
.124 .160 .128 .102 .093 .113 .373
.058 .049 .038 .067 .050 .053 .038 .192
.051 .053 .036 .046 .026 .059 .051 .062 .139
LA
```

DEPRESS EFFORT SLEEP LONELY EATING SAD GOING UNFRIEND DISLIKE
MO LX=IN TD=IN
LK
NEGATIVE SOCIAL
OU

Note that in the LISREL command file 5 for Ho. D, the MO Line of the second group (Whites) specifies that both factor loadings (LX = IN) and measurement errors (TD = IN) are invariant—that is, they are the same between the two comparative groups.

Group Goodness of Fit Statistics (African-Americans)
Contribution to Chi-Square = 81.82
Percentage Contribution to Chi-Square = 33.78

RMR = 0.022
Standardized RMR = 0.053
GFI = 0.96

Global Goodness of Fit Statistics

Degrees of Freedom = 68
Minimum Fit Function Chi-Square = 242.25 (**p = 0.0**)

RMSEA = 0.058
90% Confidence Interval for RMSEA = (0.050 ; 0.066)
p-Value for Test of Close Fit (RMSEA < 0.05) = 0.046

NNFI = 0.97
CFI = 0.97

Group Goodness of Fit Statistics (Whites)
Contribution to Chi-Square = 160.43
Percentage Contribution to Chi-Square = 66.22

RMR = 0.014
Standardized RMR = 0.040
GFI = 0.97

The last hypothesis to be tested is Ho. E.

Ho. E. The factor variances and covariances of the nine CESD items are equivalent between African-Americans and Whites.

Following is the LISREL command file for Ho. E, the MO line in Group 2 (Whites) is "MO LX = IN TD = IN PH = IN."

Command File 6.
FACTORIAL EQUIVALENCE CFA 9 CESD ITEMS: HO E
GROUP 1: OLDER BLACK
DA NI=9 NO=471 NG=2
CM
.411
.195 .535
.170 .178 .502
.202 .175 .182 .429
.138 .124 .171 .172 .463
.209 .168 .155 .231 .140 .382
.190 .224 .185 .185 .138 .198 .469
.088 .062 .079 .091 .055 .089 .084 .286
.078 .067 .082 .088 .070 .105 .086 .155 .223
LA
DEPRESS EFFORT SLEEP LONELY EATING SAD GOING UNFRIEND DISLIKE
MO NX=9 NK=2
LK
NEGATIVE SOCIAL
FR LX 2 1 LX 3 1 LX 4 1 LX 5 1 LX 6 1 LX 7 1 LX 9 2
VALUE 1 LX 1 1 LX 8 2
OU
CFA 9 CESD ITEMS TWO FACTOR MODEL OLDER WHITE
DA NI=9 NO=1099
CM
.328
.166 .425
.119 .098 .492
.167 .119 .103 .345
.100 .125 .081 .085 .332
.177 .115 .111 .161 .085 .325
.124 .160 .128 .102 .093 .113 .373
.058 .049 .038 .067 .050 .053 .038 .192
.051 .053 .036 .046 .026 .059 .051 .062 .139
LA
DEPRESS EFFORT SLEEP LONELY EATING SAD GOING UNFRIEND DISLIKE
MO LX=IN TD=IN PH=IN
LK
NEGATIVE SOCIAL
OU

Group Goodness of Fit Statistics (African-Americans)
Contribution to Chi-Square = 129.04
Percentage Contribution to Chi-Square = 40.53

RMR = 0.046
Standardized RMR = 0.14
GFI = 0.94
Global Goodness of Fit Statistics
Degrees of Freedom = 71
Minimum Fit Function Chi-Square = 318.36 ($p = 0.0$)

RMSEA = 0.069
90% Confidence Interval for RMSEA = (0.062 ; 0.076)
p-Value for Test of Close Fit (RMSEA < 0.05) = 0.00

NNFI = 0.95
CFI = 0.96

Group Goodness of Fit Statistics (White)
Contribution to Chi-Square = 189.32
Percentage Contribution to Chi-Square = 59.47

RMR = 0.022
Standardized RMR = 0.067
GFI = 0.96

The LISREL command files are presented as examples for the testing of factor structural invariance, as suggested by Joreskog and Sorbom (2001).

Reporting the Results of Cross-Cultural Hypotheses

The information of goodness-of-fit statistics concerning the five equivalence-of-factor structure hypotheses seems overwhelmed and unnecessary. They are reported here for the sole purpose of illustration and to help the readers become familiar with the LISREL outputs. Analysts should report at least two tables from the results of a cross-cultural evaluation of factor structure equivalence. One table is for the within-group CFA, including factor loadings and error measurements of the scale for each group (*see* Table 7.1). The other table is the summary of goodness-of-fit tests for each of the five hypotheses (*see* Table 7.2). Following are examples of these two tables derived from the aforementioned analyses.

Table 7.1 Within-Group CFA With a Two-Factor Model for Nine CESD Items

| Scale items | African-Americans (n = 471) | | | | Whites (n = 1099) | | | |
| | Negative | | Social | | Negative | | Social | |
	ML^a (δ)	CSS (δ)	ML (δ)	CSS (δ)	ML (Error)	CSS (δ)	ML (δ)	CSS (δ)
Depress	1.00	0.69			1.00	0.76		
	(0.22)	(0.53)			(0.14)	(0.43)		
Effort	0.93	0.56			0.85	0.56		
	(0.37)	(0.69)			(0.29)	(0.68)		
Sleep	*0.89*	0.56			*0.67*	**0.41**		
	(0.35)	(0.69)			(0.41)	(0.83)		
Lonely	*1.06*	0.71			*0.86*	**0.64**		
	(0.21)	(0.76)			(0.20)	(0.59)		
Eating	**0.76**	0.49			0.58	**0.43**		
	(0.35)	(0.76)			(0.27)	(0.81)		
Sad	1.04	0.74			*0.90*	0.68		
	(0.17)	(0.45)			(0.17)	(0.54)		
Going	*0.99*	0.64			*0.73*	0.52		
	(0.28)	(0.59)			(0.27)	(0.73)		
Unfriendly			1.00	0.72			1.00	0.59
			(0.14)	(0.48)			(0.14)	(0.43)
Dislike			**1.04**	0.85			**0.92**	**0.64**
			(.06)	(0.27)			(0.17)	(0.59)

Goodness-of-Fit Statistics

Minimum fit function chi-square (DF) 49.24 (26) (p = 0.00)[b] 142(26) (p = 0.00)[b]

$RMSEA^c$	0.044	0.065
$NNFI^c$	0.98	0.95
GFI^c	0.98	0.97
$AGFI^c$	0.96	0.95

[a] ML = maximum likelihood estimates; error = Theta-Delta; CSS = completely standardized solution;
[b] The p-value of this test should be greater than 0.05.
[c] RMSEA with a value less than 0.05 indicates good fit; NNFI, GFI, and AGFI with a value close to 0.95 indicate good fit (Schumacher & Lomax, 2004).

Without testing any hypothesis of factor structure equivalence between African-Americans and Whites, the evidence from the within-group CFA results show that both factor loadings and measurement errors of the nine CESD items exhibit differences in both values and magnitudes between African-Americans and Whites. All reported measures of fit appear to be more favorable for African-Americans than for Whites.

Summary Results of the Assessment of Measurement Invariance

Following is the example of a summary table for the testing of five factor-structure equivalence hypotheses. Table 7.2 presents the results from the testing of five measurement equivalence hypotheses. This table should be presented after the information of within group comparisons (*see* Table 7.1).

Table 7.2 Assessing Measurement Invariance Hypotheses for the CFA Model With Two Factors

Model & Hypothesis	χ^2 (DF)	$\Delta\chi^2$	RMSEA	NNFI	CFI	ΔCFI
A. Omnibus Model	167.45(45)					
B. Baseline Model & Factor Pattern Invariance	191.27(52)		0.060	0.97	0.97	
C. Factor Loading Invariance	204.54(59)	13.27(7)^{ns}	0.057	0.97	0.97	0.00
D. Measurement Error Invariance	242.25(68)	37.71(9)	0.058	0.97	0.97	0.00
E. Factor Variance & Covariance Invariance	318.36(71)	76.11(3)	0.069	0.95	0.96	−0.01

^{ns} $p > 0.05$

Notes:

$\chi2$ (DF) and $\Delta\chi2$. Difference values of $\chi2$ and associated degrees of freedom between nested models (e.g., MC-MB, MD-MC, ME-MD) should have a $p > 0.05$ to accept the hypothesis of Invariance.

Root-mean-square error of approximation (RMSEA): The value should be less than 0.05 and no greater than 0.08 (Vanderberg & Lance, 2000).

NNFI (TLI: Tucker-Lewis Index): The value should be equal to or greater than 0.90 and closer to or equal 1.00 (Jan-Benedict & Baumgartner, 1998).

Comparative fit index (CFI): The value should be greater than 0.90 and closer to or equal 1.00 (Jan-Benedict & Baumgartner, 1998).

Δ CFI: Changes in CFI values from nested models should be −0.01 or less. Changes lie between −0.01 and −0.02 suggest differences (Vanderberg & Lance, 2000).

Interpretation

The results in Table 7.2 are mixed. Although the $\Delta\chi2$ between the metric invariance (factor loading invariance) and the baseline model (factor pattern invariance) is not statistically significant ($\Delta\chi2$ [7DF] $= 13.27$, $p > 0.05$), the values of RMSEA range between 0.057 and 0.060, suggesting a relatively weak measurement invariance. It is possible that the factor pattern is weak in both groups. Because these nine items were drawn from a well-established scale that has more than two factors (Radloff, 1977, 1991), it is possible that these measurement invariances will improve when the items are specified to represent three or four factors.

Stacked Command Files

In the aforementioned examples, Hypotheses C, D, and E can be tested in a single analysis. The LISREL command files of these three hypotheses can be stacked together in one file as follows:

Command File 7
```
FACTORIAL EQUIVALENCE CFA 9 CESD ITEMS: HO C
GROUP 1: OLDER BLACK
DA NI=9 NO=471 NG=2
CM
.411
.195 .535
.170 .178 .502
.202 .175 .182 .429
.138 .124 .171 .172 .463
.209 .168 .155 .231 .140 .382
.190 .224 .185 .185 .138 .198 .469
.088 .062 .079 .091 .055 .089 .084 .286
.078 .067 .082 .088 .070 .105 .086 .155 .223
LA
DEPRESS EFFORT SLEEP LONELY EATING SAD GOING UNFRIEND DISLIKE
MO NX=9 NK=2
LK
NEGATIVE SOCIAL
FR LX 2 1 LX 3 1 LX 4 1 LX 5 1 LX 6 1 LX 7 1 LX 9 2
VALUE 1 LX 1 1 LX 8 2
OU
```

```
FACTORIAL EQUIVALENCE CFA 9 CESD ITEMS: HO C
GROUP 2: OLDER WHITE
DA NI=9 NO=1099
CM
.328
.166 .425
.119 .098 .492
.167 .119 .103 .345
.100 .125 .081 .085 .332
.177 .115 .111 .161 .085 .325
.124 .160 .128 .102 .093 .113 .373
.058 .049 .038 .067 .050 .053 .038 .192
.051 .053 .036 .046 .026 .059 .051 .062 .139
LA
DEPRESS EFFORT SLEEP LONELY EATING SAD GOING UNFRIEND DISLIKE
MO LX=IN
LK
NEGATIVE SOCIAL
OU
FACTORIAL EQUIVALENCE CFA 9 CESD ITEMS: HO D
GROUP 1: OLDER BLACK
DA NI=9 NO=471 NG=2
CM
.411
.195 .535
.170 .178 .502
.202 .175 .182 .429
.138 .124 .171 .172 .463
.209 .168 .155 .231 .140 .382
.190 .224 .185 .185 .138 .198 .469
.088 .062 .079 .091 .055 .089 .084 .286
.078 .067 .082 .088 .070 .105 .086 .155 .223
LA
DEPRESS EFFORT SLEEP LONELY EATING SAD GOING UNFRIEND DISLIKE
MO NX=9 NK=2
LK
NEGATIVE SOCIAL
FR LX 2 1 LX 3 1 LX 4 1 LX 5 1 LX 6 1 LX 7 1 LX 9 2
VALUE 1 LX 1 1 LX 8 2
OU
CFA 9 CESD ITEMS TWO FACTOR MODEL OLDER WHITE: HO D
```

```
DA NI=9 NO=1099
CM
.328
.166 .425
.119 .098 .492
.167 .119 .103 .345
.100 .125 .081 .085 .332
.177 .115 .111 .161 .085 .325
.124 .160 .128 .102 .093 .113 .373
.058 .049 .038 .067 .050 .053 .038 .192
.051 .053 .036 .046 .026 .059 .051 .062 .139
LA
DEPRESS EFFORT SLEEP LONELY EATING SAD GOING UNFRIEND DISLIKE
MO LX=IN TD=IN
LK
NEGATIVE SOCIAL
OU
FACTORIAL EQUIVALENCE CFA 9 CESD ITEMS: HO E
GROUP 1: OLDER BLACK
DA NI=9 NO=471 NG=2
CM
.411
.195 .535
.170 .178 .502
.202 .175 .182 .429
.138 .124 .171 .172 .463
.209 .168 .155 .231 .140 .382
.190 .224 .185 .185 .138 .198 .469
.088 .062 .079 .091 .055 .089 .084 .286
.078 .067 .082 .088 .070 .105 .086 .155 .223
LA
DEPRESS EFFORT SLEEP LONELY EATING SAD GOING UNFRIEND DISLIKE
MO NX=9 NK=2
LK
NEGATIVE SOCIAL
FR LX 2 1 LX 3 1 LX 4 1 LX 5 1 LX 6 1 LX 7 1 LX 9 2
VALUE 1 LX 1 1 LX 8 2
OU
CFA 9 CESD ITEMS TWO FACTOR MODEL OLDER WHITE: HO E
DA NI=9 NO=1099
CM
```

.328
.166 .425
.119 .098 .492
.167 .119 .103 .345
.100 .125 .081 .085 .332
.177 .115 .111 .161 .085 .325
.124 .160 .128 .102 .093 .113 .373
.058 .049 .038 .067 .050 .053 .038 .192
.051 .053 .036 .046 .026 .059 .051 .062 .139
LA
DEPRESS EFFORT SLEEP LONELY EATING SAD GOING UNFRIEND DISLIKE
MO LX=IN TD=IN PH=IN
LK
NEGATIVE SOCIAL
OU

Revising the Specifications of the Confirmatory Factor Analysis Model

It should be noted that any set of observed items can have more than one measurement model as long as each latent factor has a minimum number of two observed items (Jan-Benedict & Baumgartner, 1998). These nine items of the CESD scale can have no more than four latent factors. In revising the measurement specifications of the observed items, researchers should be guided by theory, clinical observations, and the pattern of the interitem correlation among the observed variables. To provide the readers with more examples of CFA models and factor-structures equivalence analysis for cross-cultural comparisons, three- and four-factor CFA models are illustrated in the remainder of this chapter.

A Confirmatory Factor Analysis Model with Three Factors for Nine CESD Items

Table 7.3 presents the new specifications of the nine CESD items. This table specifies that these nine items will be loaded on three factors (latent constructs): negative feelings, somatic complains, and social relationship problems. The relationships between the nine observed items and their three respective factors are described here.

Figure 7.3 demonstrates the CFA diagram of nine CESD items and their three factors.

Table 7.3 Description of the Relationship Between Nine CESD
Items and Three Factors

Items	Negative	Somatic	Social
1. I felt **depressed**.	X		
2. I felt that everything I did was an **effort**.		X	
3. My **sleep** was restless.		X	
4. I felt **lonely**.	X		
6. I did not feel like **eating**; my appetite was poor.		X	
7. I felt **sad**.	X		
9. I could not get "**going**."		X	
5. People were **unfriendly**.			X
8. I felt that people **dislike** me			X

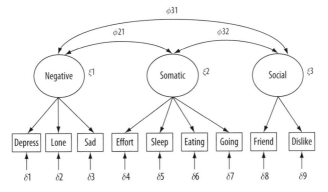

Figure 7.3 Confirmatory Factor Analysis Model for Nine CESD
Items with Three Factors

LISREL Command Files and Results for Within-Group Confirmatory Factor Analysis

Before assessing the cross-cultural equivalence in the measurement properties of the revised CFA model, it is always important to perform a within-group CFA for each selected group. The command file is similar to the command file for the CFA with two factors. The key differences are the specifications of the number of latent factors and the relationships between the observed items and the latent factors. In the MO line, the command file specifies three latent variables (NK = 3), whereas the number of observed items remains the same (NX = 9). The summary results of the CFA for African-Americans will be reported side by side with the CFA for Whites (*see* http://www.oup.com/us for the complete command files).

Summary Results for Within-Group Confirmatory Factor Analysis

Table 7.4 presents the summary statistics for two separated CFA models: African-Americans and Whites. This table contains information

Table 7.4 Within-Group CFA for African-Americans and Whites With A Three-Factor Model

Latent factors	African-Americans ($n = 471$)		Whites ($n = 1099$)	
	ML[a] (δ)	CSS (δ)	ML (δ)	CSS (δ)
Negative				
Depressed	1.00	0.69	1.00	0.78
	(0.21)	(0.52)	(0.13)	(0.40)
Lonely	1.07	0.72	0.86	0.65
	(0.20)	(0.47)	(0.20)	(0.57)
Sad	1.06	0.76	0.90	0.70
	(0.16)	(0.42)	(0.16)	(0.50)
Somatic				
Effort	1.00	0.59	1.00	0.64
	(0.35)	(0.65)	(0.25)	(0.59)
Sleep	0.96	0.59	0.74	0.44
	(0.33)	(0.66)	(0.20)	(0.57)
Eating	0.79	0.50	0.67	0.48
	(0.35)	(0.75)	(0.25)	(0.77)
Going	1.07	0.68	0.88	0.60
	(0.25)	(0.54)	(0.24)	(0.64)
Social				
Unfriendly	1.00	0.72	1.00	0.59
	(0.14)	(0.48)	(0.12)	(0.65)
Dislike	1.04	0.85	0.92	0.64
	(0.06)	(0.28)	(0.08)	(0.59)

Goodness-of-Fit Statistics

*Minimum fit function chi-square (24 DF) = 35.69 (**p = 0.06**)[b]*		75.10 ($p = 0.00$)
Root-mean square error of approximation (RMSEA) = 0.033		0.044
NNFI[c]	0.99	0.98
GFI[c]	0.98	0.99
AGFI[c]	0.97	0.97

[a] ML = maximum likelihood estimates; error = Theta-Delta; CSS = completely standardized solution.

[b] The p-value of this test should be greater than 0.05.

[c] RMSEA with a value less than 0.05 indicates good fit; NNFI, GFI, and AGFI with a value close to 0.95 indicate good fit (Schumacher & Lomax, 2004).

regarding unstandardized factor loadings and their associated measurement errors, completely standardized factor loadings and their associated measurement errors, and key goodness-of-fit statistics.

The results of two within-groups CFA have indicated that the CFA model of nine CESD items appears to fit the data of African-Americans better than Whites. The minimum fit function chi-square with 24 degrees of freedom for both groups is not significant for African-Americans ($p = 0.06$), but it is statistically significant for Whites ($p = 0.00$). However, these two within-group CFAs do not allow researchers to test any hypotheses of cross-cultural equivalence of the factor structures of the nine CESD items between African-Americans and Whites.

Assessing Equivalence of Measurement Properties of the Confirmatory Factor Analysis Model with Three Factors

The analyses of the equivalence of the CFA model with three factors are similar to those of the two factors. The LISREL command files for the testing of five basic hypotheses of equivalent factor structures between the two groups are also similar (*see* http://www.oup.com/us for the complete command file). Table 7.5 presents the summary statistics of these five hypotheses.

Interpretation

The summary statistics in Table 7.5 indicate that the three-factor model of nine CESD items has strong measurement equivalence regarding the conceptualization of the factor pattern and the corresponding factor loadings. The chi-square difference between the metric equivalence model and the baseline model is not significant, indicating an equivalence in the factor loadings of these nine items between African-Americans and Whites ($\Delta \chi 2$ [6 DF] $= 10.63, p > 0.10$). Compared to the results in Table 7.2 of the two-factor CFA model, this CFA model offers a better validity and reliability. More specifically, the values NNFI and CFI in the baseline model and the metric equivalence model are similar and stable.

Table 7.5 Assessing Measurement Invariance Hypotheses for the CFA Model With Three Factors

Model & Hypothesis	χ^2 (DF)	$\Delta\chi^2$	RMSEA	NNFI	CFI	ΔCFI
A. Omnibus Model	167.45(45)					
B. Baseline Model & Factor Pattern Invariance	110.79(48)		0.04	0.98	0.99	
C. Factor Loading Invariance	121.42(54)	$10.63(6)^{ns}$	0.05	0.98	0.99	0.00
D. Measurement Error Invariance	165.42(63)	$44(9)^*$	0.04	0.98	0.98	−0.01
E. Factor Variance & Covariance Invariance	244.22(69)	$78.8(6)^*$	0.06	0.97	0.97	−0.01

^{ns} $p > 0.10$
* $p < 0.05$

Notes:

χ^2 (DF) and $\Delta\chi^2$. Difference values of χ^2 and associated degrees of freedom between nested models (e.g., MC-MB, MD-MC, ME-MD) should have a $p > 0.05$ to accept the hypothesis of Invariance.

Root-mean square error of approximation (RMSEA): The value should be less than 0.05 and no greater than 0.08 (Vanderberg & Lance, 2000).

NNFI (TLI: Tucker-Lewis Index): The value should be equal to or greater than 0.90 and closer to or equal 1.00 (Jan-Benedict & Baumgartner, 1998)

Comparative fit index (CFI): The value should be greater than 0.90 and closer to or equal 1.00 (Jan-Benedict & Baumgartner, 1998)

Δ CFI: Changes in CFI values from nested models should be –0.01 or less. Changes lie between –0.01 and –0.02 suggest differences (Vanderberg & Lance, 2000).

A Confirmatory Factor Analysis Model With Four Factors for Nine CESD Items

Table 7.6 presents the specification of nine CESD items and their respective four factors: negative feelings, lack of energy, somatic complains, and social relationship problems. Table 7.6 presents the maximum number of factors of the nine CESD items. As noted earlier, each factor must have no less than two observed items.

Confirmatory Factor Analysis Model for Nine CESD Items With Four Factors

As described in Table 7.6, the maximum number of latent factors that these nine CESD items can account for is four factors. Negative factor

Table 7.6 Description of the Relationship Between Nine CESD Items and Four Factors

Items	Negative	Energy	Somatic	Social
1. I felt **depressed.**	X			
2. I felt that everything I did was an **effort.**		X		
3. My **sleep** was restless.			X	
4. I felt **lonely.**	X			
6. I did not feel like **eating**; my appetite was poor.			X	
7. I felt **sad.**	X			
9. I could not get "**going.**"		X		
5. People were **unfriendly.**				X
8. I felt that people **dislike** me				X

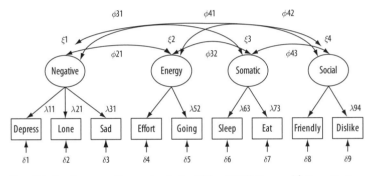

Figure 7.4 Confirmatory Factor Analysis of Nine CESD Items with Four Factors

encompasses three items, and each of the remaining factors (lack of energy, somatic complaints, and social relationship) has two items.

Figure 7.4 is the CFA diagram of nine CESD items with four factors.

The LISREL command files for within-group CFA for African-Americans and Whites can be found at http://www.oup.com/us.

Table 7.7 presents the summary of LISREL results for of CFA for African-Americans and Whites.

The four-factor CFA model for nine CESD items appears to fit the data among African-Americans very well compared with the two- and three-factor CFA models. The chi-square for the four-factor CFA model for African-Americans has a probability value of 0.20 ($p = 0.20$) compared with the three-factor CFA model ($p = 0.06$) and the two-factor

Table 7.7 CFA for Nine CESD Items With Four Factors for African-Americans and Whites

| Latent factors | African-Americans (n = 471) | | Whites (n = 1099) | |
	ML^a (δ)	CSS (δ)	ML (δ)	CSS (δ)
Negative				
Depressed	1.00	0.69	1.00	0.77
	(0.21)	(0.52)	(0.13)	(0.44)
Lonely	1.07	0.72	0.87	0.65
	(0.20)	(0.47)	(0.20)	(0.57)
Sad	1.06	0.76	0.91	0.70
	(0.16)	(0.42)	(0.16)	(0.50)
Energy				
Effort	1.00	0.62	1.00	0.66
	(0.33)	(0.61)	(0.24)	(0.57)
Going	1.08	0.72	0.87	0.61
	(0.23)	(0.48)	(0.23)	(0.62)
SOMATIC				
Sleep	1.00	0.64	1.00	0.43
	(0.30)	(0.59)	(0.40)	(0.82)
Eating	0.83	0.55	0.89	0.47
	(0.32)	(0.69)	(0.26)	(0.78)
Social				
Unfriendly	1.00	0.72	1.00	0.59
	(0.14)	(0.48)	(0.13)	(0.65)
Dislike	1.05	0.85	0.93	0.64
	(0.04)	(0.27)	(0.08)	(0.59)

Goodness-of-Fit Statistics

Minimum fit function chi-square (21 DF) = 26.13 ($p = 0.20$)[b]   71.60 (P = .00)
Root-mean square error of approximation (RMSEA) = 0.022   0.047
NNFI[c]   1.00   0.97
GFI[c]   0.99   0.99
AGFI[c]   0.97   0.97

[a] ML = maximum likelihood estimates; error = Theta-Delta; CSS = completely standardized solution.
[b] The p-value of this test should be greater than 0.50.
[c] RMSEA with a value less than 0.05 indicates good fit; NNFI, GFI, and AGFI with a value close to 0.95 indicate good fit (Schumacher & Lomax, 2004).

CFA model ($p = 0.00$). Both RMSEA and NNFI measures of fit are stronger for African-Americans than for Whites. None of the CFA models for Whites has a probability value greater than 0.05.

Assessing Equivalence of Measurement Properties of the Confirmatory Factor Analysis Model with Four Factors

The LISREL command files for the testing of the equivalence of factor structures between African-Americans and Whites for Hypothesis A (equal covariance matrices) is the same as those of the two- and three-factor CFA models. There are differences in the MO lines for Hypotheses B (equal-factor pattern), C (equal-factor loadings), D (equal-measurement errors), and E (equal-factor variance and covariance). The MO lines for these hypotheses are listed in the following paragraphs.

Hypothesis B (African-Americans)
MO NX=9 NK=4
LK
NEGATIVE ENERGY SOMATIC SOCIAL
FR LX 4 1 LX 6 1 LX 7 2 LX 5 3 LX 9 4
VALUE 1 LX 1 1 LX 2 2 LX 3 3 LX 8 4
Hypothesis B (Whites)
MO LX=PS
Hypotheses C (African-Americans)
MO, LK, FR, and VALUE lines are the same as of Ho B.
Hypothesis C (Whites)
MO LX=IN (C)
Hypothesis D (African-Americans)
MO, LK, FR, and VALUE lines are the same as of Ho B
Hypothesis D (Whites)
MO LX=IN TD=IN (D)
Hypothesis E (African-Americans)
MO, LK, FR, and VALUE lines are the same as of Ho B
Hypothesis E (Whites)
MO LX=IN TD=IN PH=IN (E)

The readers can replace these specifications with those in the LISREL command files for the three-factor CFA model to produce the following summary statistics for the five hypotheses concerning the equivalence of the four-factor CFA model between African-Americans and Whites. Table 7.8 presents the summary results of these five hypotheses concerning the equivalence of the four-factor CFA model between African-Americans and Whites.

Table 7.8 Assessing Measurement Invariance Hypotheses for the CFA Model With Four Factors

Model & Hypothesis	$\chi2(DF)$	$\Delta\chi2$	RMSEA	NNFI	CFI	ΔCFI
A. Omnibus Model	167.45(45)					
B. Baseline Model & Factor Pattern Invariance	97.81(42)		0.04	0.98	0.99	
C. Factor Loading Invariance	107.24(47)	$9.43(5)^{ns}$	0.04	0.98	0.99	0.00
D. Measurement Error Invariance[a]	144.88(56)	$37 (12)^*$	0.04	0.98	0.98	-0.01
E. Factor Variance & Covariance Invariance	235.50(66)	$90.63(10)^*$	0.06	0.97	0.97	-0.01

[a] This model has a warning: Because PH is not definitely positive, this indicates poor data or identification problems.

[ns] $p > 0.09$

[*] $p < 0.05$

Notes:

$\chi2$ (DF) and $\Delta\chi2$ (difference values of $\chi2$ and associated degrees of freedom between a nested model [e.g., Metric Invariance Model and the Subsequent Models] and the Baseline Model) should have a $p > 0.05$ to accept the hypothesis of Invariance.

Root-mean-square error of approximation (RMSEA): The value should be less than 0.05 and no greater than 0.08 (Vanderberg & Lance, 2000).

NNFI (TLI: Tucker-Lewis Index): The value should be equal to or greater than 0.90 and closer to or equal 1.00(Jan-Benedict & Baumgartner, 1998).

Comparative fit index (CFI): The value should be greater than 0.90 and closer to or equal 1.00 (Jan-Benedict & Baumgartner, 1998).

Δ CFI: Changes in CFI values from nested models should be -0.01 or less. Changes lie between -0.01 and -0.02 suggest differences (Vanderberg & Lance, 2000).

Interpretation

The results in Table 7.8 indicate that the CFA model of nine CESD items with four factors also has weak cross-cultural equivalence in its factor pattern and factor loadings between African-Americans and Whites. However, when imposing invariance for the measurement errors between the two groups, there are possible problems with the data or identification. Therefore, the three-factor model is recommended over the four-factor model.

These examples of factor structure equivalence analyses illustrate the applications of CFA using LISREL for cross-cultural social work research. Although these examples used real data, the readers should not attempt to draw any meaningful conclusions concerning the measurement properties of these nine CESD items. The specifications for these nine items in the examples were not based on any extensive theoretical framework or clinical observations. The readers should only use these examples as the guide for their own cross-cultural evaluations of measurement equivalence with their own data or research projects.

The aforementioned examples are based on LISREL's recommended procedures (Joreskog & Sorbom, 2001). One can also perform cross-cultural measurement invariance, as suggested by Steenkamp and Baumgartner (1998). They recommended a six-step approach for the testing or evaluating measurement invariance: *(1)* configural invariance, *(2)* metric invariance, *(3)* scalar invariance, *(4)* factor covariance invariance, *(5)* factor variance invariance, and *(6)* error invariance.

Configural Invariance

This is an assumption that the observed items or indicators should possess the same configuration of pattern of salient (nonzero) and nonsalient (zero or approximately zero) factor loadings across different cultural groups (Horn & McArdle, 1992).

Metric Invariance

Although the configuration invariance requires that a concept is measured by the same number of factors or dimensions, it does not require that the observed items or indicators of a concept have the same relationships (factor loadings) with their respective factors or latent variables. Metric invariance implies that each observed item has the similar factor loading on it respective factor across different cultural groups.

Scalar Invariance

Metric invariance does not warrant the observed items have the same distribution of scores across groups (Meredith, 1995). If the purpose of the cross-cultural research project is to compare the mean of a concept across cultural groups, then it is necessary to assume that the intercepts of the observed items are similar across the comparative groups.

Factor Covariance Invariance

This test implies that the covariance of factors in a multidimensional scale or measure is similar across groups.

Factor Variance Invariance

This test can be undertaken for both uni- and multidimensional scales. The test assumes that variance accounted for by each factor is similar across groups.

Invariance of the correlations among factors across cultural groups can be established if the scale has similar factor covariances and factor variances.

Error Variance Invariance

Each observed item or indicator of a measure or scale often consists of some degrees of unexplained variance or measurement error. The test for error variance invariance implies the observed items of a measure have similar measurement errors across different cultural groups.

The combination of metric invariances, factor invariances, and error invariances across cultural groups is an indication of good cross-cultural reliability (Steenkamp & Baumgartner, 1998).

Full and Partial Invariance

The likelihood that a measure or a scale has full or complete measurement invariance is often unlikely (Horn, 1991, Horn, McArdle & Mason, 1983). Researchers have suggested that partial invariance is acceptable for cross-cultural comparisons (Lastovicka, 1982; Byrne, Shavelson & Muthen, 1989; Reise, Widaman & Pugh, 1993). A scale of 10 items may have only six items that are invariant across the comparative groups.

In this case, researchers can impose measurement invariance for those six items and relax the other four. This is considered partial invariance. Modification indices (MIs) and expected parameter changes (EPCs) can help researchers identify an item that might be relaxed from invariant constraints. The rule of thumb is that items with the greatest MI and substantial EPC should be relaxed in an incremental manner. Each factor must have at least two items that have equal factor loadings and item intercepts for meaningful mean comparison across groups (Steenkamp & Baumgartner, 1998).

Testing Equivalence of Factor Correlation and Factor Means

Finally, one can also test for the cross-cultural equivalence of factor correlation and factor means (latent means) across groups. If there are strong reasons to believe that the correlation among the factors (latent dimensions) and the means of the factors (latent means) differ across groups, then one can test these two hypotheses using LISREL procedures. Followings are two sample command files.

Command File 8: Equivalence of Factor Correlation

The purpose of the following command file is to test the hypothesis that the correlations of three factors encompassing nine observed items of the CESD scale are correlated in the same manner and magnitude between African-Americans and Whites.

```
TESTING FACTOR CORRELATION EQUIVALENCE CFA 9 CESD ITEMS 3 FACTORS:
GROUP 1: OLDER BLACK
DA NI=9 NO=471 NG=2
CM
.411
.195 .535
.170 .178 .502
.202 .175 .182 .429
.138 .124 .171 .172 .463
.209 .168 .155 .231 .140 .382
.190 .224 .185 .185 .138 .198 .469
```

```
.088 .062 .079 .091 .055 .089 .084 .286
.078 .067 .082 .088 .070 .105 .086 .155 .223
ME
1.53 1.74 1.64 1.51 1.27 1.53 1.49 1.21 1.65
LA
DEPRESS EFFORT SLEEP LONELY EATING SAD GOING UNFRIEND DISLIKE
MO NX=9 NK=3 PH=FI
LK
NEGATIVE SOMATIC SOCIAL
FR LX 1 1 LX 4 1 LX 6 1 LX 2 2 LX 3 2 LX 5 2 LX 7 2 LX 8 3 LX 9 3 PH 2 1 PH 3 2 PH 3 1
VALUE 1 PH 1 1 PH 2 2 PH 3 3
OU
GROUP 2: OLDER WHITE
TESTING FACTOR CORRELATION EQUIVALENCE CFA 9 CESD ITEMS 3 FACTORS:
DA NI=9 NO=1099
CM
.328
.166 .425
.119 .098 .492
.167 .119 .103 .345
.100 .125 .081 .085 .332
.177 .115 .111 .161 .085 .325
.124 .160 .128 .102 .093 .113 .373
.058 .049 .038 .067 .050 .053 .038 .192
.051 .053 .036 .046 .026 .059 .051 .062 .139
ME
1.38 1.51 1.68 1.36 1.16 1.30 1.37 1.12 1.53
LA
DEPRESS EFFORT SLEEP LONELY EATING SAD GOING UNFRIEND DISLIKE
MO PH=IN
FR LX 1 1 LX 4 1 LX 6 1 LX 2 2 LX 3 2 LX 5 2 LX 7 2 LX 8 3 LX 9 3
OU
```

In the above command file, the covariance matrix is specified as fixed in the first group (PH = FI). All factor loadings (LX) are specified as free estimates. The variances of the factors are assigned a value of 1, and the covariances are specified as free estimates (FR PH 2 1 PH 3 2 PH 3 1). In the second group, the correlations among the factors are specified as invariant (PH = IN). This implies that the correlations among the three factors among Whites are expected to be the same with those of

African-Americans. Because of space limitations, no results are reported here. The readers can execute this command file as an exercise. The chi-square test of significance is used to test the hypothesis. If the probability of this test is greater than 0.05, the conclusion is that the correlations among the factors are the same between the comparison groups. The results from the above command file reveals that the hypothesis of equal factor correlations is rejected based on the chi-square statistics (global goodness of fit : minimum fit function chi-square $= 116.78$, degrees of freedom $= 51$, $p = 0.00$).

The following command file is for the testing of the hypothesis of equal latent means (factor means). Researchers can test whether a one- or multidimensional scale has similar factor means cross cultural groups.

Command File 9: Equivalence of Factor Means

```
FACTORIAL MEANS EQUIVALENCE CFA 9 CESD ITEMS 3 FACTORS:
GROUP 1: OLDER BLACK
DA NI=9 NO=471 NG=2
CM
.411
.195 .535
.170 .178 .502
.202 .175 .182 .429
.138 .124 .171 .172 .463
.209 .168 .155 .231 .140 .382
.190 .224 .185 .185 .138 .198 .469
.088 .062 .079 .091 .055 .089 .084 .286
.078 .067 .082 .088 .070 .105 .086 .155 .223
ME
1.53 1.74 1.64 1.51 1.27 1.53 1.49 1.21 1.65
LA
DEPRESS EFFORT SLEEP LONELY EATING SAD GOING UNFRIEND DISLIKE
MO NX=9 NK=3 TX=FR KA=FI
LK
NEGATIVE SOMATIC SOCIAL
FR LX 4 1 LX 6 1 LX 3 2 LX 5 2 LX 7 2 LX 9 3
VALUE 1 LX 1 1 LX 2 2 LX 8 3
OU TV SS ND=2
GROUP 2: OLDER WHITE
```

```
FACTORIAL MEANS EQUIVALENCE CFA 9 CESD ITEMS 3 FACTORS: HO B
DA NI=9 NO=1099
CM
.328
.166 .425
.119 .098 .492
.167 .119 .103 .345
.100 .125 .081 .085 .332
.177 .115 .111 .161 .085 .325
.124 .160 .128 .102 .093 .113 .373
.058 .049 .038 .067 .050 .053 .038 .192
.051 .053 .036 .046 .026 .059 .051 .062 .139
ME
1.38 1.51 1.68 1.36 1.16 1.30 1.37 1.12 1.53
LA
DEPRESS EFFORT SLEEP LONELY EATING SAD GOING UNFRIEND DISLIKE
MO LX=IN TX=IN KA=FR TD=IN
OU
```

In the above command file, the intercepts of the factor items are specified to be free estimates (TX = FR), and the factor means are fixed
estimates (KA = FI) in the first group. In the second group, the command file specifies that the factor loadings (LX = IN), item intercepts
(TX = IN), and measurement errors (TD = IN) are invariant from those
of the first group. However, the factor means (KA = FR) are specified as
free estimates. Because of space limitations, only the mean differences
and the chi-square test of goodness of fit are reported. The following
matrix of KAPPA (means) reveals that differences in the latent means of
the three factors are statistically significant between African-Americans
and Whites, in that Whites have significantly lower means of negative feelings, somatic complaints, and social relationship problems than
African-Americans.

```
KAPPA

    KSI 1      KSI 2      KSI 3
    ----       ----       ----
   −0.18      −0.14      −0.11
   (0.03)     (0.03)     (0.02)
   −6.28      −4.52      −4.65
```

The chi-square test of significance indicates that the hypothesis of equal-factor means are rejected (global goodness of fit : minimum fit function chi-square $= 205.64$, degrees of freedom $= 69$, $p = 0.00$).

This chapter offers several hands-on examples of using LISREL CFA and multisample analyses of factor structures as the tools to evaluate cross-cultural equivalence in the measurement properties of the research instruments, whether they are newly developed or translated from a source language. The chapter briefly mentions the issue of "partial invariance," which can be easily done once the readers are familiar with the general multisample analysis approach illustrated in this book. In addition to the testing of five traditional hypotheses of factor structure invariance, the readers are also provided with examples for the testing of factor correlations and factor means across groups.

8

Concluding Comments
Measurement in Cross-Cultural Research

This book is about the processes and techniques of cross-cultural instrument development. Most of its contents and discussion are about cross-cultural research within a diverse society, such as the United States. However, the issues and techniques discussed in the book can be used in cross-national research. The term culture should be understood from micro- and macrolevels. Microlevel refers to the study of different subgroups within a society or a community. These subgroups can be identified by their race, ethnicity, religion, gender, language, and even political orientation. At the macrolevel, cross-cultural analyses can be viewed as the comparison of different nations and continents. In the following concluding comments, the readers are reminded of the key issues and techniques that were covered throughout this book. There are also recommendations for social work researchers to confront the critical issues concerning evidence-based practices in cross-cultural settings.

In Chapter 1, readers are introduced to the field of cross-cultural research from multidisciplinary perspectives. Although the chapter offers a brief review of anthropology, psychology, political science, and sociology, cross-cultural research can be found in other fields such as communication, health and mental health, and marketing. In general, all of these fields have to confront the same issue of cross-cultural equivalence of research instruments. Regardless of the research questions or interests, no cross-cultural comparison is valid without having equivalent research measures or instruments. Using other cross-cultural research disciplines, social work research can draw their theories, paradigms, and methods as guides for its own research and evaluations in cross-cultural settings. From anthropology, social work can learn from its extensive body of research on cultures and experiences in conducting field research. From psychology, social work can borrow its theories on cultural values and personality and how these theories can help social work with designing and implementing cross-cultural interventions. As globalization has become a fact of life for many nations and continents, its impacts definitely have both positive and negative effects on the well-being of all citizens of the world. Political science can help social work understand how political systems change and how they are related to other social institutions in human societies. Finally, from sociology, social work can draw from sociological theories such as functionalism and modernization in its attempts to confront social problems that are consequences of the breakdown of social systems at all levels and the changes from traditions to modern and postmodern societies.

The overall process of cross-cultural instrument development was presented and discussed in Chapter 2. The key points of this chapter are:

1. Meaningful and feasible research aims can only be developed with the participation of all stakeholders.
2. The decision of adopting or adapting existing instruments is guided by the research aims with consensus from key research personnel and representatives from the research populations.
3. The development of a new instrument is time-consuming and costly.
4. Different approaches of evaluation, including expert evaluation, cognitive interviews, focus groups, and field pilot surveys must be the integral parts of cross-cultural instrument development.

There are basic preparations that require attention from the research team prior to the development of a cross-cultural research instrument. Chapter 3 provides recommendations for the foundation of a good research instrument development team, including criteria for recruiting cultural experts, translators, focus group moderators, interviewers, and participants for cognitive interviews and focus groups. A competent research support team and qualified participants will warrant the quality of a cross-cultural instrument.

If the research team decides to adopt or adapt existing instruments, the translation of the existing instruments into the target languages is crucially important for the success the research project. Chapter 4 illustrates a cross-cultural translation process with practical recommendations and data highlighting the potential sources of biases in cross-cultural research.

Chapter 5 explains the process of developing new research instruments. The readers are introduced to the foundation of measurement theory and the necessary process of identifying and defining the research concepts. The readers learn to ascertain the relationships between the latent variables and their observed indicators. Key research methods, including cognitive interviews, focus groups, expert groups, and pilot surveys, are explained and illustrated with practical recommendations.

Chapter 6 provides the readers with some basic statistical approaches to evaluate cross-cultural reliability and validity of the research instruments. This chapter uses existing cross-cultural data to illustrate the applications of descriptive statistics in cross-cultural evaluations of reliability and validity. The readers learn to examine the distribution and response pattern of the items on a scale or an index across cultural groups. In addition, the readers are guided with examples of how to use internal consistency analysis and exploratory factor analysis to examine the reliability and validity of a research instrument across groups.

In Chapter 7, the author uses real data to illustrate and explain the application of LISREL confirmatory and multisample confirmatory factor analysis as the key approaches to evaluate the fundamental psychometric properties of a research instrument within and across cultural groups. Researchers have used different techniques to evaluate cross-cultural equivalence of reliability and validity of the research instruments (Hui & Triandis, 1985); however, the LISREL multisample confirmatory factor analysis approach has been widely recognized as the most powerful technique in the testing of measurement invariance across groups (Joreskog, 1971; Jan-Benedict & Baumgartner; 1988). If the readers replicate the examples in Chapter 7, they will have a fairly strong foundation and practical tools to carry out their own cross-cultural evaluations of reliability and validity of cross-cultural research instruments. Although this chapter illustrates the application of LISREL, the readers will be able to make a transition in learning how to use other statistical software for the same purpose (Byrne, 2001; Reise, Keith & Pugh, 1993).

Similarly to other approaches of analyses, there are no universal or gold standards in cross-cultural research, especially in cross-cultural instrument developments and constructions. This book offers social work researchers and students a basic guide for cross-cultural instrument development and evaluation. Both descriptive statistical approaches and LISREL multisample confirmatory factor analyses are demonstrated and illustrated to give the readers the necessary tools to conduct further analyses in cross-cultural validity and reliability of research instruments.

As a practical guide for social work researchers who plan to conduct cross-cultural instrument development for research and evaluation, this book does not discuss statistical techniques from statistical theory and principles. The author presents several hands-on examples with data to illustrate the application of these statistical techniques for cross-cultural assessment of measurement equivalence across cultural groups.

It is very expensive to develop cross-cultural research instruments. However, this should not discourage or deter social work researchers from moving forward with their attempts or endeavors to establish acceptable cross-cultural research instruments for practice evaluation and hypothesis testing.

All social work practice and research are culturally based because we are living in a time of rapid globalization of business and human migration. The undesirable consequences of using nonequivalent research instruments in cross-cultural social work practice and research outweigh the cost of instrument development. Incorrect screening instruments or bias diagnostic procedures lead to false implementation of treatments, and false treatments can harm clients socially, psychologically and financially. Cross-cultural measurement development requires the researchers to be aware of cultural nuances of the target culture. A research concept or variable must be defined in the context of the target culture.

Researchers should consider gender differences within the target culture at every step of the instrument development. When an instrument is developed for two or more cultural groups, representatives of these groups must be invited to participate in the research process from the formulation of the research questions, conceptualization and operationalization of research variables, to questionnaire construction and interpretation of the results. This process is also equally important for the development of social work treatments and programs. Prospective clients should be invited to design and evaluate treatments and programs. Social work treatments and programs must bear similar purposes, implementation, and expected outcomes across different cultural groups.

When researchers decide to adopt or adapt existing research instruments for a cross-cultural research project, there must be efforts to bring in experts and prospective respondents or clients from the target cultural groups to evaluate the utility of the borrowed instruments in the contexts of the comparative cultures. Focus groups, cognitive interviews, cultural translation procedures, field tests, and pilot tests should be employed to assess the adaptability and efficacy of the borrowed instruments in cross-cultural contexts before they can be implemented.

Quantitative evaluations of cross-cultural equivalence of the research instruments play a major role in the assessment of measurement equivalence across cultural groups. Descriptive analyses of data distribution and internal consistency of the observed items can be performed with small pilot samples. Exploratory factor analysis, confirmatory factor analysis, and multigroup confirmatory factor analysis require larger sample sizes. These analyses should be performed at the last stage of instrument development process.

Researchers should re-evaluate the cross-cultural comparability of the research instruments after the completion of the final research or evaluation projects. Information from field evaluation and pilot tests are not sufficient to arrive with the affirmation of cross-cultural equivalence of the research instruments or variables. If necessary, some items that exhibit serious cultural nonequivalence in their measurement properties can be dropped from the final analyses.

LISREL multigroup confirmatory factor analysis is not the only statistical method for assessing cross-cultural equivalence of measurement properties of the research instruments. The readers can use the Item Response Theory method to assess cultural comparability of the observed items of research instruments across different cultural groups. The discussion of this topic is beyond the scope of this book (Ostini & Nering, 2005; Embretson, 1991). The needs for cross-cultural research in social work remain unfulfilled in both methodologies and substantive areas. Given the diverse nature of the client populations, social work researchers can no longer ignore the importance of using cross-culturally reliable and valid research instruments in their research.

Cross-Cultural Evidence-Based Social Work

As the issues of evidence-based social work have become increasingly important in social work, cross-cultural equivalence in every aspect of social work practice and research will be a matter of interest among social workers and researchers. Perhaps the most challenging issue in cross-cultural research is the equivalence of research instrument or measurement. Cultural equivalence in the treatment and outcome measure becomes equally important for both practitioners and researchers. Although it is fair to say that we can never establish absolute cultural equivalence for the interventions and outcome measures, it is important to realize that without an acceptable level of cross-cultural equivalence in the treatment and outcome measures, there is no valid comparison of the treatment efficacy among different cultural groups. For social work, cultural equivalence must be reflected in interventions, the process of intervention implementations, and outcomes. If a treatment has different meanings and is being implemented differently among cultural groups, then there is no meaningful comparison of its effectiveness.

For a treatment to be comparable across different cultural or ethnic groups, the treatment should have the following components:

Equivalent psychosocial disease or problem
Equivalent target population
Equivalent treatment goals and objectives
Equivalent treatment activities or treatment components
Equivalent treatment frequency and intensity
Equivalent treatment implementation
Equivalent treatment outcome measures

Equivalent Psychosocial Disease or Problem

This refers to the notion that a disease or social, psychological condition must be recognized across different cultural or ethnic groups. Both clients and social workers from different cultural backgrounds must have a similar understanding of the nature of a disease or social, psychological condition that requires similar treatments. There must be equivalence in the definition and manifestation of a social or psychological disease before a treatment can be implemented for clients of different cultures. If depression is a universal psychiatric disease, then its definition and symptomatic indicators must be understood and agreed upon by mental health professionals and clients across different cultural or ethic groups before a selected treatment can be implemented.

Equivalent Target Population

This refers to the notion that the clinician is able to identify the right target population for a specific treatment. If the treatment is designed for depression, the clinician must use the same depression screening instrument or diagnostic procedure to identify the right clients or patients across cultural or ethnic groups.

Equivalent Treatment Goals and Objectives

This requires that a treatment must have similar goals and objectives for clients regardless of their cultural backgrounds. Because these goals and objectives will be used to determine the treatment outcomes, if goals and objectives of a treatment are different across client groups, it is difficult to compare the effectiveness or efficacy of such a treatment among different client groups or populations.

Equivalent Treatment Activities or Treatment Components

This requires that the treatment activities and processes be similar across different cultural groups of clients. All clients should be treated in the exact manner or protocol from the beginning to the end of a treatment.

Equivalent Treatment Frequency and Intensity

This requires that social workers give the same number of treatment sessions and the same amount of time for each treatment session to all involved clients with similar diagnostic conditions, regardless of their cultural or ethnic backgrounds.

Equivalent Treatment Implementation

This requires that all social workers execute or implement a treatment in the same manner for all involved clients. It is also assumed that social workers receive similar training on the use of a particular treatment and have similar credentials and knowledge of the treatment and client population.

Equivalent Treatment Outcome Measures

This requires that social workers use the same outcome measures to evaluate the expected outcomes of a particular treatment across different client populations. The selected outcome measure must have similar reliability and validity among the comparative client groups.

The above criteria are ideal. In reality, social workers must do their best to serve their clients. It is crucially important for social workers to be mindful of cultural differences among their clients and act accordingly in their attempts to modify existing interventions.

This book also aims to help social workers become critical consumers of research involving cross-cultural comparisons. There is no doubt that the readers will end this book with more questions about cross-cultural social work research than answers. This book does not provide solutions to all issues of cross-cultural social work research and evaluation. The field of cross-cultural social work research is wide open, and there are needs for more contributions in both theory and methodology.

Followings are three general suggestions that cross-cultural social work researchers may consider in the design and implementation of a cross-cultural research or evaluation project.

The Importance of Community Involvement

The ultimate purpose of social work research and evaluations is to improve the quality of life of individuals and community at all levels. Whether the researchers aim to test theoretical hypotheses or evaluate the effectiveness of a treatment or program, it is always important to involve the community throughout the process of their research or evaluation projects. In a cross-cultural research project, researchers should create a council of cultural advisors that will provide guidance and input for the conceptualization of the research ideas, development of research instruments, recruitment of research subjects, and interpretation and dissemination of the results.

Use Multimethod of Cross-Cultural Translation

Translation of survey instruments from one language to other languages should be treated with the utmost consideration. If the translated version of the research instrument fails to capture its original meaning, then the results are not comparable or valid. For example, if one translates a depression scale from English to a target language and the meaning of the translated version of the scale ends up measuring anxiety, then the translated version lost its original validity and, therefore, is not appropriate for any cross-cultural comparison. As a result, one should always use more than one method of translation and evaluation (e.g., back-translation, group translation, cognitive interviews, focus groups, expert evaluation, and pilot testing) to warrant the original validity and the comparability of the translated instrument.

Gender Importance

Cross-cultural social work researchers should take gender difference into consideration throughout the process of translation of the research instrument. There is no doubt that men and women from different cultures exhibit different patterns of oral and written communication (Costa, 1994). Previous studies have confirmed the important role of gender in communication (Ostini & Nering, 2005; Embretson, 1991). Thus, researchers should involve equal numbers of female and male translators in the instrument translation process to avoid gender biases in translation and the use of language in their social interactions.

Finally, in the culturally diverse society of the United States, social work research should conduct research on two or more cultural groups. Because of the fact that people from different cultural backgrounds often have different life situations that consequently will impact their well-being. Social work research should investigate how these diverse groups manifest their psychological status. Each cultural group may have different pathways to social and psychological problems and illness. The lack of knowledge on the development of problems and illness could prevent social workers from finding the appropriate resources and interventions. These types of research questions require social work researchers to develop effective cross-cultural research instruments. This book offers some practical guides for social work researchers to confront many timely and important issues in cross-cultural social work research and evaluation.

Cross-Cultural Data Resources

Social work researchers and students can visit the following Web sites to search for existing data archives for exercises or research. These Web sites contain a rich data source for cross-cultural analyses of various health, mental health, and social issues that are relevant to social work.

World Health Organization
http://www.who.int/en/
Social Sciences Virtual Library
http://www.dialogical.net/socialsciences/directories.html
Australian Social Science Data Archive
http://assda.anu.edu.au/
Inter-University Consortium for Political and Social Research
http://www.icpsr.umich.edu/

References

Agans, R.P., Deeb-Sossa, & Kalsbeek, W.D. (2006). Mexican immigrants and the use of cognitive assessment techniques in questionnaire development. Hispanic Journal of Behavioral Sciences, 28, 209–230.

Anderson, C.., Hughes, S.O., Fisher, J., & Nicklas, T.A. (2005). Cross-cultural equivalence of feeding beliefs and practices: The psychometric properties of the child feeding questionnaire among Blacks and Hispanics. Preventive Medicine, 41, 521–531.

Bentler, P.M. (1976). Factor analysis. In P.M. Bentler, D.J Lettieri & G.A. Austin (Eds.), Data Analysis Strategies and Design for Substance Abuse Research (pp. 139–158). Washington, DC: U.S. Government Printing Office.

Barkow, G., Cosmides, L., & Tooby, J. (Eds.) (1992). The Adapted Mind: evolutionary Psychology and the Generation of Culture. New York: Oxford University Press.

Bean, F.D. & Stevens, G. (2003). America's Newcomers and the Dynamics of Diversity. New York: Russell Sage Foundation.

Berg, B.L (2004). Qualitative Research Methods for the Social Sciences. Boston: Pearson.

Berry, J.W. & Triandis, H.C. (2004). Cross-Cultural Psychology, Overview. In C.D. Spielberger (Ed.), Encyclopedia of Applied Psychology, Volume 1, A-E. Oxford, UK: Elsevier, pp. 527–538.

Berry, J.W., Poortinga, Y.H., Segall, M.H., & Dasen, P.R. (1992). Cross-cultural psychology: Research and Applications. Cambridge: Cambridge University Press.

Blalock, H.M. (1971). Causal models involving unobserved variables in stimulus-response situations. In H.M. Blablock (Ed.). *Causal Models in the Social Sciences* (pp. 335–347). Chicago: Aldine.

Brislin, R.W., Lonner, W.J., & Throndike, R.M. (1973). *Cross-Cultural Research Methods*. New York: John Wiley & Sons.

Bollen, K.A. (1989). *Structural Equations with Latent Variables*. New York: John Wiley & Sons.

Bollen, K. and Lennox, R. (1991). Conventional wisdom on measurement: A structural equation perspective. Psychological Bulletin, 110, 305–314.

Byrne, B.M. (1998). *Structural Equation Modeling with LISREL, PRELIS, and SIMPLIS: Basic Concepts, Applications, and Programming*. New Jersey: Lawrence Erlbaum Associates.

Byrne, B.M. (2001). *Structural Equation Modeling with AMOS: Basic Concepts, Applications, and Programming*. New Jersey: Lawrence Erlbaum Associates.

Byrne, B.M. (1995). Strategies in testing for an invariant second-order factor structure: A comparison of EQS and LISREL. Structural Equation Modeling A Multidisciplinary Journal, 2, 53–72.

Byrne, B.M., Shavelson, R.J., & Muthen, B. (1989). Testing the equivalence of factor covariance and mean structures: The issue of partial measurement invariance. Psychological Bulletin, 105, 456–466.

Burton, M.L. & White, D.R. (1987). Cross-cultural surveys today. Annual Review of Anthropology, 16, 143–160.

Cameron, D. (1988). Gender, language, and discourse: A review essay. Signs: Journal of Women in Culture and Society, 23, 954–1073.

Chao, G.T. & Moon, H. (2005). The cultural mosaic: a tetatheory for understanding the complexity of culture. Journal of Applied Psychology, 90, 1128–1140.

Child, D. (1990). *The Essentials of Factor Analysis, Second Edition*. London: Cassel Educational Limited.

Collins, D. (2003). Protesting survey instruments: An overview of cognitive methods. Quality of Life Research, 12, 229–238.

Converse, J. & Pressner, S. (1986). *Survey Questions: Handcrafting the Standardized Questionnaire*. Newbury Park, CA: Sage.

Costa, J.A. (Ed.) (1994). *Gender Issues and Consumer Behavior*. Thousand Oaks, CA: Sage.

Costello, A.B. & Osborne, J.W. (2005). Best practices in exploratory factor analysis: Four recommendations for getting the most from your analysis. Practical Assessment, Research & Evaluation, 10, 1–9.

Cronbach, L.J. & Meehl, P.E. (1955). Construct validity in psychology tests. Psychological Bulletin, 52, 281–302.

Corsini, R.J. (1999). *The Dictionary of Psychology*. Philadelphia, PA: Brunner/Mazel.

Cote-Arsenault, D. & Morrison-Beedy, D. (1999). Practical Advise for Planning and Conducting Focus Groups. Nursing Research, 48, 280–283.

CSWE (2001). Educational Policy and Accreditation Standards. http://www.cswe.org/CSWE/. June 20, 2008.

Davis, K. (1997). National survey of Hispanic Elderly people, 1988 (ICPSR 9289). Ann Arbor, MI.: Inter-University Consortium for Political and Social Research.

Deng, X., Doll, W., Hendrickson, A., & Scazzero, J.A. (2005). A multi-group analysis of structural invariance: an illustration using the technology acceptance model. Information and Management, 42, 745–759.

DeVellis, R.F. (1991). Scale Development: Theory and Applications. Newbury Park: Sage.

Edwards, J.R. & Bagozzi, R.P. (2000). On the Nature and directions of Relationships between Construct and Measures. Psychological methods, 5, 155–174.

Embretson, S.E. (1991). Item Response Theory for Psychologists. Thousand Oaks, CA: Sage.

Fabrigar, L.R., Wegener, D.T., MacCallum, R.C., & Strahan, E.J. (1999). Evaluating the use of exploratory factor analysis in psychological research. Psychological Methods, 4, 272–299.

Fayers, P.M. & Machin, D. (2007). Quality of Life: The Assessment, Analysis and Interpretation of Patient-Reported Outcomes, Second Edition. West Sussex, England: Wiley.

Fowler, F.J., Jr. & Cannell, C.F. (1996). Using Behavioral Coding to Identify Cognitive Problems with Survey Questions. In N. Schwarz & S. Sudman (Eds.), Answering Questions: Methodology for Determining the Cognitive and Communicative Processes in Survey Research. San Francisco: Jossey-Bass, pp. 15–36.

Fornell, C. & Bookstein, F.L. (1982). Two structural equation models: LISREL and PLS applied to consumer exit voice theory. Journal of Marketing Research, 19, 440–452.

Forsyth, B.H., Levin, K., & Fisher, S.K. (1999). Test of an appraisal method for establishment survey questionnaires. Proceedings of the Section on Survey Research Methods, American Statistical Association, 145–149.

Grimshaw, A.D. (1973). Comparative sociology: In what ways different from other sociologies? In M. Armer & A.D. Grimshaw (Eds.), Comparative Social Research: Methodological Problems and Strategies. New York: John Wiley & Sons, pp. 3–48.

Green, J. (Ed.). (1982). Cultural Awareness in the Human Services. Englewood Cliffs, NJ: Prentice Hall.

Guillemin, F., Bombardier, C., & Beaton, D. (1993). Cross-cultural adaptation of health-related quality of life measures: Literature review and proposed guidelines. Journal of Clinical Epidemiology, 46, 1417–1432.

Harkness, J. (2003). Chapter 3: Questionnaire translation. In J.A. Harkness, J.R. Fons Van de Vijver, & P. Ph. Mohler (Eds.), *Cross-Cultural Survey Methods*. Wiley-Interscience, A John Wiley & Sons Publication, New Jersey, pp. 35–56.

Harkness, J., Pennell, B.E., & Schoua-Glusberg, A. (2004). Questionnaire translation and assessment. In Presser, S., Rothgeb, J., Couper, M., Lessler, J., Martin, J., & Singer, E. (Eds.), *Methods for Testing and Evaluating Survey Questionnaires*. New Jersey: John Wiley and Sons, pp. 453–473.

Hui. C.H. & Triandis, H.C. (1985). Measurement in cross-cultural psychology: A review and comparisons of strategies. Journal of Cross-Cultural Psychology, 16, 131–152.

Hauser, R.M. (1973). Disaggregation a social psychological model of educational attainment. In A.S. Goldberger & O.D. Duncan (Eds.), *Structural Equation Models in the Social Sciences*. San Diego, CA.: Academic Press, pp. 255–289.

Hoelter, J.W. (1983). Factorial invariance and self-esteem: Reassessing Race and Sex Differences. Social Forces, 61, 835–846.

Hofstede, G. (1980). *Culture's Consequences: International Differences in Work-Related Values*. Newbury Park, CA: Sage.

Horn, J.L. & McArdle, J.J. (1992). A practical and theoretical guide to measurement invariance in aging research. Experimental Aging Research, 18, 117–144.

Horn, J.L. (1991), Comments on Issues in Factorial Invariance. In Best Methods for the Analysis of Change, Ed., Linda M. Collins and John L. Horn. Washington, D.C. American Psychological Association, 114–125.

Horn, J.L., McArdle, J., & Mason, R. (1983). When is invariance not invariant: A practical scientist's look at the ethereal concept of factor invariance. The Southern Psychologist, 1, 179–188.

House, J.S. (2006). American's Changing Lives: Waves I, II, and III, 1986, 1989, and 1994 (ICPSR Study No. 3394). Ann Arbor, MI: ICPSR.

Inglehart, R. & Baker, W.E. (2000). Modernization, cultural change, and the persistence of traditional values. American Sociological Review, 65, 19–51.

Inglehart, R. & Abramson, P.R. (1999). Measuring postmaterialism. American Political Science Review, 93, 665–677.

Jorgensen, J.G. (1979). Cross-cultural comparisons, Annual Review of Anthropology, 8, 309–331.

Krueger, R.A. (1988). *Focus Groups: A Practical Guide for Applied Research*. Newbury Park, CA: Sage.

Krueger, R.A. (1994). *Focus Groups: A Practical Guide for Applied Research (2nd ed.)*. Thousand Oaks, CA:

Kazdin, A.E. (2000). *Encyclopedia of Psychology*. Washington, D.C.; New York: American Psychological Association. Oxford: Oxford University Press.

Kim, J.O. & Mueller, C.W. (1978). *Factor Analysis: Statistical Methods and Practice Issues*. Newbury Park, CA: Sage.

Kluckhohn, C. (1954). Culture and Behavior. In G. Lindzey (Ed), *Handbook of Social Psychology, Volume 2*, Cambridge, MA: Addison-Wesley, pp. 921–976.

Kohn, M.L. (1987). Cross-national research as an analytic strategy: American Sociological Association, 1987 Presidential Address. American Sociological Review, 52, 713–731.

Lastovicka, J.L. (1982). On the validation of lifestyle traits: A review and illustration. Journal of Marketing Research, 19, 126–138.

Lessler, J.T. & Forsyth, B.H. (1996). A coding system for appraising questionnaires. In N. Schwarz and S. Sudman (eds.), *Answering Questions*. San Francisco, CA: Jossey-Bass, pp. 259–291.

Li, R.M., McCardle, P., Clark, R.L., Kinsella, K., & Berch, D. (Eds.) (2001). *Diverse Voices—Inclusion of Language-Minority Populations in National Studies: Challenges and Opportunities. National Institute on Aging and National Institute of Child Health and Human Development.* http://www.nichd.nih.gov/publications/pubs/upload/Diverse_Voices.pdf. Bethesda, MD.

Liang, J. et al. (2005). How does self-assessed health change with age? A study of older adults in Japan. Journal of Gerontology: Social Sciences, 60(4), S224–S232.

Lubove, R. (1965). The professional altruist: The emergence of social work as a career. Cambridge, MA: Harvard University Press.

McCrea, R.R. & John, O.P. (1992). An introduction to the five factor model and its applications. Journal of Personality, 60, 175–215.

Malpass, R.S. (1997). Theory and method in cross-cultural psychology. American Psychologist, 32, 1069–1079.

Maneesriwongul, W. & Dixon, J.K. (2004). Instrument translation process: A methods review. Journal of Advanced Nursing, 48, 175–186.

MacCallum, R.C. & Browne, M.W. (1993). The use of causal indicators in covariance structure models: Some practical issues. Psychological Bulletin, 114, 533–541.

Martin, E. (2006). Survey questionnaire construction: Survey methodology #2006-12. U.S. Census Bureau. Washington, D.C.

Martin, E. (2004). Vignettes and respondent debriefing for questionnaire designs and evaluation. In S. Presser, J.M. Rothgeb, M.P. Couper, J.L. Lessler, E. Martin, J. Martin, and E. Singer (Eds.). Methods for Testing and Evaluating Survey Questionnaires, New York: Wiley.

Marsella, A.J., Dubanoski, J., Hamada, W.C., & Morse, H. (2000). The measurement of personality across cultures: Historical, conceptual, and methodological issues and considerations. American Behavioral Scientist, 44, 41–62.

Meredith, W. (1995). Two wrongs may not make a right. Multivariate Behavioral Research, 30, 89–94.

Morgan, D.L. (1988). Focus Groups As Qualitative Research. New Bury Park, CA: Sage.

Nader, L. (2000). Anthropology! Distinguished Lecture-2000. American Anthropologist, 103, 609–620.

NASW (2001). NASW Standards for cultural competence in social work practice. Washington, D.C.: NASW.

Nunnally, J. (1978). Psychometric Theory, Second Edition. New York: McGraw-Hill.

NIST/SEMATECH e-Handbook of Statistic Methods, http://ww/itl.nist.gov/div898/handbook. June 17, 2008.

Jahoda, G. & Krewer, B. (1997). History of cross-cultural and cultural psychology. In J.W. Berry, Y.H.Poortinga, & J. Pandey (Eds.) Handbook of Cross-Cultural Psychology: Theory and Method, Volume 1. Boston: Allyn and Bacon, pp. 1–42.

Joreskog, K. & Sorbom, D. (2001). LISREL 8: User's Reference Guide. Lincolnwood, IL: Scientific Software International Inc.

O'Brien, E., Fisher, S., Goldenberg, K., & Rosen, R. (2001). Application of cognitive method to an establishment survey: A demonstration using the current employment statistics survey. Proceeding of the Annual Meeting of the American Statistical Association, August 5-10, 2001.

Ostini, R.D. & Nering, M.L. (2005). Polytomous item response theory model. Thousand Oaks, CA: Sage.

Poortinga, Y.H. (1989). Equivalence of cross-cultural data: An overview of basic issues. International Journal of Psychology, 24, 737–756.

Pedhazur, El.J. & Schmelkin, L.P. (1991). Measurement, Design, and Analysis: An Integrated Approach. Hillsdale, New Jersey: Lawrence Erlbaum Associates.

Pen, Y. & Puente, M. D.L. (2005). Census Bureau Guideline for the translation of data collection instruments and supporting materials: Documentation on how the guideline was developed. Research Report Series: Survey Methodology #2005-06. Washington DC: Statistical Research Division, U.S. Bureau of the Census.

Pye, L.E. (1997). The elusive concept of (political) culture and the vivid reality of Personality. Political Psychology, 18(2), 241–254.

Radloff, L.S. (1977). The CESD Scale: A Self-Report depression Scale for Research in the General Population. Applied Psychological Measurement, 1, 385–401.

Radloff, L.S. (1991). The Use of the Center for Epidemiologic Studies Depression Scale in Adolescents and Young Adults. Journal of Youth and Adolescence, 20(2), 149–166.

Raykov, T. & Marcoulides, G.A. (2006). *A First Course in Structural Equation Modeling (2nd Ed.)*. Mahwah, NJ: Lawrence Erlbaum Associates.

Reise, S.P., Keith, F.W., & Pugh, R.H. (1993). Confirmatory factor analysis and item response theory: Two approaches for exploring measurement invariance. Psychological Bulletin, 114, 552–566.

Robinson, L. (2000). Multi-cultural Society, Social Work Practice in a. In M. Davies & R. Barton (Eds.), *The Blackwell Encyclopedia of Social Work*. Malden, MA: Blackwell Publishers, pp. 222–223.

Rothgeb, J., Willis, G., & Forsyth, B. (2005). Questionnaire pretesting methods: Do different techniques and different organizations produce similar results? Research Report Series (Survey Methodology #2005-02). Statistical research Division. U.S. Census Bureau, Washington, D.C.

Schaeffer, N.C. & Presser, S. (2003). The Science of Asking Questions. Annual Review of Sociology, 29, 65–88.

Schumacker, R.E. & Lomax, R.G. (2004). *A Beginner's Guide to Structural Equation Modeling, second edition*. Mahwah, New Jersey: Lawrence Erlbaum Associates, Publishers.

Schwartz, N. & Oyserman, D. (2001). Asking questions about behavior: Cognition, communication, and questionnaire construction. American Journal of Evaluation, 22, 127–160.

Sugisawa, H., Shibata, H., Hougham, G., Sugihara, Y., & Liang, J. (2002). The impact of social ties on depressive symptoms in U.S. and Japanese elderly. Journal of Social Issues, 58, 785–804.

Salzman, P.C. (2001). *Understanding Culture: An Introduction to Anthropology Theory*. Prospect heights, Ill: Waveland Press.

Shin, H.B. & Bruno, R. (October 2003). Language use and English-speaking ability: 2000. Census Brief. U.S. Department of Commerce, Economics and Statistics Administration, U.S. census Bureau. Retrieved from http://www.census.gov/prod/2003pubs/c2kbr-29.pdf on 2/15/05.

Singer, M. (1968). Culture. In D.L. Sills (Ed.) *International Encyclopedia of the Social Sciences*. New York: The Macmillan Company & The Free Press, pp. 527–543.

Smith, T.W. (2004). Cross-national survey research: the challenge and promise. ICPSR Bulletin, XXIV, 3–12.

Stewart, D.W. & Shamdasani, P.N. (1990). *Focus Groups: Theory and Practice*. Newbury Park, CA: Sage.

Steinhoff, P.G. (2001). Area and international studies: Sociology. In N.J. Smelser & P.B. Baltes (Eds.), *International Encyclopedia of the Social and Behavioral Sciences*. Oxford: Elsevier Science Ltd., pp. 723–729.

Stokoe, E. & Smithson, J. (2001). Making gender relevant: Conversation analysis and gender categories in interaction. Discourse and Society, 12, 217–244.

Tabachnick, B.G. & Fidel, L.S. (2001). *Using Multivariate Statistics*. Boston: Allyn and Bacon.

Thompson, B. (2004). *Exploratory and Confirmatory Factor Analysis: Understanding Concepts and Applications*., Washington, D.C.: American Psychological Association.

Tomlinson, J. (1999). *Globalization and Culture*. Cambridge: Polity Press.

Tran T.V., Khatutsky, G., Aroian, K.J., Balsam, A., & Convey, K. (2000). Living Arrangements, and Health Status Depression Among Russian Elderly Immigrants, Journal of Gerontological Social Work, 33(2), 63–77.

Tran, T.V., Ngo, D., & Conway, K. (2003). A cross-cultural measure of depressive symptoms among Vietnamese Americans. Social Work Research, 27, 56–64.

Tylor, E.B. (1857, 1958). *The Origins of Culture*. New York: Harper and Row.

United Nations. (2002). International migration report 2002 (Document No. ESA/P/WP. 178). New York: Author.

U.S. Bureau of the Census. 2001. *The Hispanic Population 2000*. Census Brief #C2KBR/01-3. Washington, DC: US Department of Commerce.

U.S. Census Bureau (2000). Adding Diversity from abroad: the foreign-born population, 2000. Population Profile of the United States: 2000 (Internet Release).

Van de Vijver, V.D., & Leung, K. (1997). *Methods and Data Analysis for Cross-Cultural Research*. Thousand Oaks, CA: Sage.

Van Herk, H., Poortinga, Ype. H., & Verhallen, T.M.M. (2005). Equivalence of survey data: Relevance for international marketing. European Journal of Marketing, 39, 351–364.

Vandenberg, R.J. (2002). Toward a further understanding of and improvement in measurement invariance methods and procedures. Organizational Research Methods, 5, 139–158.

Vandenberg, R. J., & Lance, C.E. (2000). A review and synthesis of the measurement invariance literature: Suggestions, practices, and recommendations for organizational research. Organizational Research Methods, 3, 4–70.

Wedeen, L. (2002). Conceptualizing culture: Possibilities for Political Science. American Political Science Review, 96, 713–728.

Willis, G.B. (1999). Cognitive Interviewing: A "How To" Guide: Research Triangle Institute.

Wu, B,. Tran, T.V., & Amjad, Q.A. (2004). Chronic Illness and Depression among Chinese Elderly Immigrants. Journal of Gerontological Social Work, 43(2/3), 79–95.

Index

.